NO NOOSE IS GOOD NOOSE

By

Lawrence B. Fox

Edited by
Dianne F. Pelaggi

If you enjoy this book, you may wish to read the author's other humorous works regarding the practice of law:

There's No Justice - Just Court Costs
ISBN 09663402-2-1

Has My Lawyer Called Yet?
ISBN 0-9724891-0-X

Published in the United States by
Fox Publications, Inc.
915 West Broad Street
Bethlehem, PA 18018
Telephone: 610-861-9297
Visit our website at *www.lawrencebfox.com*

TABLE OF CONTENTS

PREFACE

This is the third book I have authored that focuses upon trials I should have won but lost, and trials I should have lost, but won. The stories are true, except where I've lied a little. Nonetheless, please note that the people and situations depicted in this book are fictitious. Any similarity to any individual living or dead is purely coincidental.

These short stories may be read by lawyer and client alike, or by anyone who believes he or she may not have received a sufficient amount of Justice at some point in life. After reading these misadventures, perhaps you won't feel so bad, as you find that the Justice you received probably far exceeded the paltry amount dished out to my luckless clients.

Each chapter consists of a separate unrelated incident. You may peruse any chapter in any order. Reading a chapter should take no more than a few minutes. If you enjoy this collection of humor, please don't hesitate to contact me. I appreciate receiving e-mail. Talk to me at: LBFox@ptd.net

Other humorous books written by me in a similar style are entitled *There's No Justice - Just Court Costs* (first published 1999) and *Has My Lawyer Called Yet?* (first published 2002). For more information, visit me on the web at *www.lawrencebfox.com*

It has always been my belief that for a story to be humorous, it must be clean. The reader won't find bad language in these chapters, nor do sexual, racial, or ethnic comments lurk among the pages. The great humorists like Jack Benny, W. C. Fields, and Bob and Ray, knew that only clean humor survives the test of time.

Some readers have criticized me, perhaps justifiably, for abruptly ending some stories in such a manner that the reader is forced to draw his own conclusions. That is my intention. In the practice of law, there are many questions, yet so few answers. If every irony described in this book were suddenly resolved by some magical wave of the judicial wand, there would be no need to write the story. The reader alone must seek his own answer.

I want to thank my tireless paralegal Cathy Rudolph for typing rewrite after rewrite; to Laura Tobey for her technical support; to imaginative Lorie Reinhard, my illustrator; and to my editor, Dianne Pelaggi. This book could not have become a reality without her common sense and insightful comments.

It is not possible to adequately thank my website friends at *www.forcounsel.com.* and *www.Amazon.com.* Back when no agent or publishing house would take my form of humor seriously, these folks took a chance and offered my books for sale. Thanks to all of you.

At Bethlehem, Pennsylvania
August 2004

DEDICATION

To every lawyer in private practice who has faced overhead on a Friday afternoon, and wasn't quite sure how to pay it...

To every lawyer in private practice who has taken a case for free because it was the right thing to do...

To every lawyer in private practice who said to his or her secretary "You're not going to believe what just happened..."

To every lawyer in private practice who has worked 12 hour days and has had to apologize to his or her family as a result...

To every lawyer in private practice who hasn't heard a funny "lawyer joke" yet...

To every lawyer in private practice who has, in the same week, been denigrated by one client and proposed for sainthood by another...

To every lawyer in private practice who has advised his clients to just tell the truth...

To every lawyer in private practice who has become a judge, but hasn't forgotten what it was like being a lawyer in private practice...

I dedicate this book.

CHAPTER 1

THE CRIME DOG

My neighbors' kids taught their dog, Phydeaux, to retrieve the morning newspaper from their front porch. It seemed like a good idea, until the obedient canine decided to collect every newspaper within a two-block radius. Dogs, in many cases, don't have a clear understanding of property rights.

Hilda Plumwort had been my client for more than 30 years. She was one of those dear old widows who worked hard, never bothered a soul, and kept out of trouble. She walked with a limp and a cane as a result of a hip replacement. The grocery store was just three blocks from her apartment of 25 years, so she never bought a car. She took the bus to church every Sunday.

"Lawyer Larry?" It was Hilda on the phone.

"Hilda? Are you O.K.?"

"Just a little shaken. I was on my way to the grocery store this morning. I needed some prunes to stew, and as I'm walking, this dog comes trotting around the corner, stops, and stares me down."

"Did he attack?" I asked.

"I'd never seen this dog before. So he comes over to me just as bold as you please, and with no warning, grabs my handbag and darts down the alley. My grocery money, my reading glasses, the keys to my apartment - they're all gone. What that mutt did - isn't that against the law?"

"It depends on whether his intentions were criminal. What did the dog look like?"

"I don't know, exactly. Black and white, or was it white and black? Medium build, short fur, I think. He came and went so fast it's hard to tell."

"Did you call the police?"

"Do they arrest dogs?"

I decided to telephone the cops. Sergeant Cranberry Hill took my call.

"That's the third complaint this week. Some dog has started doing purse snatches in the ninth ward. He only preys on the elderly, if you can believe that."

"Do you have a description of the thief?"

"There doesn't seem to be a consensus. One victim said it could have been a large white dog or perhaps a medium black one. Another poor dear thought it might be a small dog or a big cat. We're still investigating."

It was brave patrolman Roberto Lieberman who would ultimately bring the canine desperado to justice. He volunteered to dress up as a vulnerable 90-year-old nursing home escapee. He agreed to hobble down the street, dangling a handbag only a few inches above his laced orthopedic shoes. His paisley print dress covered most of his hairy legs as his full-length, silver-blue wig gleamed in the afternoon sun. The misapplied rouge on his cheeks accentuated the rhinestone rimmed bifocal glasses hanging from the chain around his neck. He faked a hip replacement limp while using a walker. An artificial alligator skin purse swung at his side.

A large black and white dog peered from around the corner, staring at its next unsuspecting prey. Lieberman clutched his purse as he inched with an unsteady gait along the sidewalk.

From out of nowhere, the villain emerged, lunged toward Lieberman, and tried to secure the purse in its powerful jaws. But this victim was different. Even though her wig fell to the ground, she wouldn't let go of her belongings. Instantaneously, the back-up patrol cars emerged, and the cops threw a dragnet over the animal, now caught red-pawed in the act of theft.

It didn't take long for the police to locate the dog's residence as the perpetrator wore up-to-date tags around its neck for rabies and distemper. Abby Mellon was arrested in his rented apartment two blocks from the scene. Three incriminating handbags and two purses were found under his bed. Not one of these fruits of crime matched any ensemble hanging in his closet, so Mellon was charged with conspiracy to commit purse snatching.

"Can someone conspire with a dog to commit a crime?" I asked assistant district attorney Purfuda Beedeldorf.

"I'll get back to you on that," she promised.

She was too busy at the moment conducting a line-up at police headquarters. All of the victims had been invited there to pick out the dog that snatched their purses. If they chose Abby Mellon's pooch, his goose was cooked.

The room with the one-way mirror was packed with spectators: cops, the assistant district attorney, the victims, and Mellon's public defender, Cyril Kocsis, Esquire.

I was there to hold Hilda's hand.

"I've never been to a line-up before," she confided.

Beebeldorf turned to the three victims.

"Now ladies, there's nothing to this. The mirror is one-sided. They can't see you from the other room, but you'll be able to see them. Each suspect has a number hanging from his neck. If you would like a specific suspect to speak or move a certain way, just let me know. O.K.?"

"O.K.," Hilda confirmed.

"O.K.," Henrietta Feather agreed as she adjusted her trifocals.

"O.K.," Murtha Grosskey chimed in as she steadied her walker.

"Bring 'em out," Beebeldorf commanded in an assistant district attorney voice drenched with authority.

Five cops led five leashed guilty-looking dogs into the line-up room. Each wore a number around its neck.

Cy Kocsis became visibly agitated. "Wait just a minute!" he interjected. "This line-up is unduly suggestive. The alleged criminal is a large black and white mutt. Four of these dogs are brown."

"I beg your pardon?" Beebeldorf responded.

"You've got a brown Chihuahua, a golden retriever, a chocolate mixed breed, and a miniature poodle in there. It's like lining up a white male suspect with a black, an Hispanic, an Asian, and an American Indian."

"Excuse me," Henrietta Feather piped up. "Could you have Number 2 step forward and bark? I think he growled before he snatched my purse. I might remember his voice."

"Have the Chihuahua step forward and speak," Beebeldorf commanded.

"I just don't know," Hilda whispered in my ear. "They all look so similar."

Three months later, Mellon went to trial. He claimed he didn't own a dog or rent an apartment, and that he had found the purses stuffed in a trashcan. The jury deadlocked. Beebeldorf may still be trying to negotiate a plea, if one of the dogs turns state's evidence.

Chapter 1
The Crime Dog

CHAPTER 2

THE BEEBELFRITZER

My office overhead keeps going up.

It was four years ago that I bought my state-of-the-art copy machine with the multiple angle enlarger, fax, correlator, stapler, with print-on-both-sides-in-color capability, and digital memory. It can send an image around the world from the touch of a button on a remote computer in two seconds flat. It can do anything. I know this even though I've never read the 70-page manual, and will never use 80% of these features.

When I first began practicing law, there were no copy machines - just carbon paper used in conjunction with hunt-and-peck typewriters. Since no image could be reproduced, offices such as the courthouse Recorder of Deeds employed a staff of ladies whose sole responsibility was to retype into the record books every word of every deed submitted for recordation.

The invention of the copy machine simplified that procedure. The clatter of courthouse typewriters ceased as images of deeds were effortlessly copied and placed on record. The reproductions, however, were unusual in one regard: The original black printed word appeared white, while the white background page was transformed into black. A small price to pay for progress.

Ultimately, private office copiers entered the market, announcing the advent of modern times at law offices worldwide. Pink translucent photo sheets were placed upon the document to be copied, and this "sandwich" was inserted into the magic machine. In less than two minutes a fuzzy image appeared on the special photographic paper, which was guaranteed not to disintegrate for up to two years. A truly efficient secretary could produce up to 20 copies an hour before it was necessary to cool down the machine's high intensity heating mechanism. That was then...

-- -- -- -- -- -- -- -- -- -

"It's the Zeenox lady on the phone," my secretary announced.

"Who?"

"She's calling about our copy machine."

"That's strange. It runs like a top. I didn't call for repairs."

I reached for the phone. The entirety of my office centered on this single machine. It was folly to keep her waiting.

"Hello," I said.

"Hi, Mr. Fox. Cindy Ragsdale, your Zeenox lady.

"Yes...Hi, Ms. Ragsdale."

"How are you?"

Uh oh! How am I? Oh, crap. Any time a salesperson asks about my well-being, it usually means I'm about to lose money "saving big" on a deal any other intelligent customer wouldn't dream of passing up.

"I'm fine," came my tentative response.

"Well, I'm calling because it's your anniversary - "

"It is?"

"Mr. Fox?"

"Yes?"

"It was four years ago you purchased your Zeenox Model B43-101-A29677038."

"Really?"

"Your 48th monthly payment was just received. For the additional payment of $1.00, you may now own the machine outright."

Free! Free at last! The Zeenox replicator duplicator B43-101-A29677038 would be mine, all mine, for just one extra dollar! The monthly payments had been higher than the installments on my first mortgage. Now I'd be able to travel, take in a show, or maybe just cut my schedule back to 60 hours a week...

"Mr. Fox?"

"Yes?"

"I have wonderful news."

"More?"

"You see, it's possible for you to save a substantial amount of money."

"I know! Without those monthly installments, I can trade in my used car and - "

"Mr. Fox..."

"Yes?"

"Now is the perfect time for you to purchase our new Zeenox Model P37-Q, the ultimate in office technology. Its computer can send satellite digital color pictures to any other similar receptor without the need for..."

"Ms. Ragsdale..."

"Yes?"

"My B43-101-A29677038 works like a charm, and for a buck I can own it. I'm finally out of debt. I don't have a need to digitally transmit images. The fax machine is sufficient. What could possibly induce me to go back into debt?"

"I'm glad you asked that question. You see, your monthly payments included a maintenance service contract. We provided 24-hour repair. But now your copier has reached its fourth birthday."

"O.K. So all I need is another service contract."

"Not exactly. See, that's where the savings come in. The monthly service contract on your outdated machine would cost more than the monthly installment on our new P37-Q. You'll save $5 per month over the next 48 months."

"But the guy who sold me my copier said it would last a lifetime!"

"Who? Bob? He's not with us any more. Repair costs are prohibitive. It's hard to find parts for obsolete machines. On the other hand, if you trade in your present antiquated - "

"Trade it in? Antiquated? I just paid the damn thing off!"

"...we can give you a credit of two monthly payments. You don't want to pass up these savings. I doubt we'll be making this offer again."

Her sales pitch was both logical and incontrovertible. It was obvious I needed a new copier, even if I didn't need one.

I reached for my dictating machine, so that I might confirm our conversation with a letter. Funny. I hadn't heard that buzzing sound before, and the mini-cassette tape wasn't supposed to unravel like that on the floor. It was good I had a 24-hour maintenance contract. The trusty service technician showed up by 3:00 p.m.

"See that?" He held up a small screw the size of a pinhead. "I think the beebelfritzer shaft is worn. How long have you had this transcriber?"

"About four years."

"Well there you go. That's a long time."

"How soon can you get me another screw?"

"Yeah, friend. See, that's a problem. Your machine is obsolete. They don't make that line of transcribulator components any more. It's bypassed by the digital scanner. Have you thought about buying a new machine?"

"But all I need is a screw!"

As I uttered those desperate words, my memory harkened back to last year's zoning hearing at the city hall rotunda. The place was packed, and with good reason. They were going to close the only hardware store left downtown, and turn it into a fast food joint. Old Heidi Frumkin was there to object.

"We need the hardware store right where it is," she pleaded frantically. "Otherwise, where are you going to get a 10 cent screw in downtown Bethlehem?"

I sensed that everyone in the hearing room was dying to tell her.

9

Chapter 2
The Beeblefritzer

CHAPTER 3

SOMEBODY OUT THERE HELP ME

I needed to go to the bathroom. It was now or never. In just 15 short minutes, Mrs. Felippa VonBushkirk would grace my law office with her presence. A patron of the arts and member of high society, Mrs. VB was dropping by to discuss her estate plan. She would probably be wearing a Queen Mother hat - one with feathers, her shoulders caressed by the pelt of a dead animal. Everything had to be perfect for her arrival. I cleaned the office. I hid the bag of potato chips, my sneakers, yesterday's newspaper, and the satchel of laundry scheduled for pick-up. Then I scooped up all the files piled on my desk, and stashed them in my secretary's office. Finally, I cleaned the fingerprints from the glass table protector, and corrected the minute hand displayed on the wind-up clock. I sprayed the room with a blanket of air freshener and headed for one last stop on the can. There was precious little time left.

I don't think I'll ever forget the insightful riddle Angelo Scott presented to me years ago: What does a man between the ages of 20 and 40 want? Sex. What does a man between the ages of 40 and 60 want? To make lots of money. What does a man between the ages of 60 and 80 want? One good crap. I'm starting to lose interest in generating legal fees. Bowel movements. That's my game.

That phrase "go to the bathroom" still makes me chuckle. I recall one co-ed hiking trip with several friends along the Appalachian Trail. One lass announced, "I have to go to the bathroom." There were no facilities within 30 miles. There were big trees, rocks and bushes to squat behind, but no place with porcelain plumbing fixtures.

Such a luxury has always stood at the ready at my law office. But unlike the hiking trail, first I have to traverse the daily mine field. Let's see...good, no incoming calls on hold. O.K. No one in the waiting room. Good...the secretaries are all busy typing. And most important, no one was standing near the bathroom door. That was it...the coast was clear!

The door issue is a subtle but incredibly important point. Unfortunately, the law office men's room door opens directly into the combination copy-kitchen-lunch room. Often the receptionist and a secretary or two or three or four will congregate there waiting for a fax. The proximity of this menagerie to the throne upon which I plan to sit is not conducive to the job at hand. The cheap wooden bathroom door, perhaps 1/2 inch thick, doesn't muffle even the faintest of bathroom sounds.

I'm not stupid. When we bought this building, I wanted to commandeer for my own what ultimately became the ladies' room. What a perfect lavatory, hidden at the end of an unused hallway. I'm the boss. So, when we bought the new law office building I exercised my omnipotent powers.

"The men will be using the bathroom at the end of the hall," I decreed.

"That'll be the day! It's ours," came the unified response from the secretaries - 4 women who had endured the indignities of a single, unisex bathroom for years at the old office.

I'll be the first to admit that the old office bathroom configuration wasn't exactly user friendly for those who expected any degree of privacy. There were very few secrets, which in a strange way, made the secretaries and lawyers feel like one big uninhibited family.

The only partition between the toilet and my private office was a wall the width of a human hair. At certain unscheduled unannounced interludes, someone, including on occasion, a client or two, might enter the rest room to answer the call of nature.

If some poor soul were constipated, had the shits, involuntarily grunted while voiding, caught his personals in his fly, or any other unspeakable scenario, I knew about it instantly, as did any unsuspecting client sitting wide-eyed across from me. During an interview, I would try to make believe nothing of significance was happening next door by raising my voice whenever Mount Vesuvius began to erupt. The smart clients did the same.

"Now Mr. Dinkelacher, do (oh no!) YOU WANT EACH OF YOUR CHILDREN TO SHARE (the bathroom groaning momentarily paused) equally in your estate?"

"Yes, but my youngest (another eruption) ISN'T 18 YET, SO HE WILL NEED (all quiet again) a trustee appointed."

It didn't matter that attempts at audio camouflage and subterfuge were employed. Some secretaries simultaneously ran the hot and cold water full blast before taking a seat. Some ran the shower as well. My law partners usually attempted to sing or whistle, usually out of tune. Nothing helped.

Over time, I became the unwitting recipient of unilateral conversational observations originating from the john, as well. Generally it was the women who would talk to themselves.

"Don't these men know enough to put the toilet seat down?" secretary after secretary would snarl. On those occasions when a fair damsel was both in a rush and in some distress, she might fail to look before she sat. What was said during these moments of waterlogged angst cannot be repeated here.

Ultimately we moved to the new office, which boasted the luxury of two separate bathrooms. It was heaven. No one would ever again know exactly when someone else reached for the toilet paper on the squeaky spindle. And we'd save a bundle on hot water. I guess it wasn't so bad that the men got the bathroom with less privacy. At least there was *some* privacy.

I needed to use the bathroom. Mrs. VonBushkirk was scheduled to arrive any minute. I dashed in, shut the door, looked first, and then sat down. Maybe I'd get done before -

"Hi. How was your weekend?"

"Short. Yours?"

Oh crap. It was the secretaries! They were gathering for their mid-morning chat outside the bathroom door. Could they hear my sounds?

"Did anyone make coffee?" Cathy asked.

Oh shit! Now there were three of them! And they were pouring coffee. My bowel gears instinctively began to turn in reverse. I couldn't go like this. I pulled up my pants and decided to make a grand exit through the copy-kitchen-lunch room and past the three hens.

Funny. I couldn't get the doorknob to turn. The carpenter had installed it only last week before we moved in. Right...left...right...left...it was stuck. I jiggled it up and down. That's when part of it, including a little metal spring, popped off, sailed through the air and disappeared down the drain of the sink. Then the knob fell off in my hand. Trapped like a rat in the bathroom, VonBushkirk on the way, part of a broken knob in my hand, and I still needed to take a dump. Another start to a perfect day here at law office Valhalla.

I politely knocked on the bathroom door.

"Is there anyone out there? I'm stuck in the bathroom. Could someone get a screwdriver and unscrew the outside doorknob? Hello?"

Silence.

Life's ironic. When intestinal fortitude has all but vanished, usually three or four ladies instinctively gather just inches from the door. Where were they all now?

I banged on the door.

"IS THERE ANYONE OUT THERE? I'M STUCK IN THE BATHROOM. I'M NOT KIDDING. DOES ANYONE HAVE A SCREWDRIVER?"

Dead silence.

There was no reason to panic. What would Agent 007 do? I had seen movies where he had been trapped - often in worse predicaments. I gathered my wits and looked around. It was simple: Just open the window, and jump out onto the back office lawn.

Funny. The window appeared to be painted shut. I'd have to loosen it. Not to worry. I picked up a handy emergency toilet plunger. I might not have a screwdriver at the ready, but with the dumps my partners took, the plunger was never very far from reach. I lightly tapped at the window frame with the wooden plunger handle. Soon I'd be free, saved by my own ingenuity.

Funny. The window was still jammed shut.

"IS THERE ANYONE OUT THERE?" I yelled in desperation. "I'M STUCK IN THE GODDAMN BATHROOM!"

Silence.

There was only one option left. I grabbed my trusty plunger and similar to a jackhammer, prepared to beat relentlessly upon the window frame. With weapon raised, I felt like a knight of old about to race toward the jousting enemy. Unfortunately, as I lunged toward my emergency escape route, I slipped on another loose spring that had rolled out from under the sink. My plunger and I missed our mark and I crashed through the window, falling headlong into a mulberry bush planted below the exterior sill. I finally came to rest on the grass next to the rear parking lot, plunger still in hand.

"Are you all right?" Mrs. VB asked as she hovered above me.

"I'm fine," I assured her as I struggled to stand while transitioning the plunger to my left hand before extending my right. "Shall we step inside to my conference room?"

"Yes," she answered. "But do you mind if I use the ladies room first?"

Chapter 3
Somebody Out There Help Me

CHAPTER 4

THE CUSTOMER IS ALWAYS RIGHT

"Uncle Clemy" was my father's best friend. They played violins together at Dad's house every Sunday for 30 years. I don't recall that the quality of their music ever changed. When they first played Mozart, the cat ran for cover. Many years later when they graduated to Mendelssohn, the cat's great-great-grandson ran for cover.

But these two musicians rarely noticed, for they knew what was truly important. If they chanced to conclude a melody at about the same time near the same measure, they would smile at each other and exhale simultaneous breaths of artistic satisfaction. Many people have spent a lifetime seeking such contentment.

When my father died, Clemy was at a loss as to how to spend his Sundays. Surprisingly, no one offered to take my father's place. That's when Clemy saw an ad for a free bus trip to Atlantic City. And it was better than free. Included was a complimentary roll of quarters for the slot machines! And so Mozart took a back seat, as did Clemy, in the Gambler's Express Motor Coach.

Clemy was old now, and it seemed no one really cared about him any more - with the exception of the attentive staff at Resorts Casino and Hotel.

Every Sunday, when he caught the bus to Atlantic City, a transformation took place. He was no longer Clemy the janitor, but "Mr. Clemson, our guest from the Lehigh Valley." Amidst the noise and the casino hustle and bustle he finally became a gentleman whose every wish deserved immediate attention and fulfillment.

He usually spent about seven hours playing the slots. Once in a while he'd try his hand at roulette. These were the only two games he understood. Blackjack, baccarat, and craps were mysteries reserved for professional gamblers. Some days he'd ride home $70 or $80 richer. Rarely had he ever made that much in a day working as a night-shift janitor for the school district. And sometimes he left in the red. But that was O.K. Even when his luck was bad, the ladies in the short skirts brought him drinks with a smile, and the 24-hour buffet had some of the best hot pastrami that side of the Pine Barrens. The other casinos simply weren't as classy or accommodating.

Clemy never married. He had no family. He retired on a full pension when he reached his 68th birthday. That was 10 years ago.

"I got tired of pushin' a broom for them kids. Forty-five years of cleaning cafeterias. And what do I have to show for it?"

I nodded in silence. "Tell me, why do you need a lawyer?"

"I was your fadder's best friend. We played music every Sunday at his house, don't you know."

"I certainly do recall. My father looked forward to those get-togethers."

"Once in a while we even gave concerts, we did!"

- - - - - - - - - - - - - - - - - - -

How very true. For a time my paternal grandfather was a resident at a nearby nursing home. My father and Clemy decided to give the old folks a treat. So the staff wheeled out about 100 old codgers into the rest home courtyard to hear some Brahms and Dvorak. I tagged along to visit my grandpa.

Dad and Clemy played non-stop for about an hour. Then the nursing staff pushed those who were still alive back into the lobby to get ready for the 4:00 p.m. dinner. Dad looked rather pleased with himself. He loved to play for an appreciative audience, although in this case, I don't recall that anyone had the strength to applaud. My father approached grandfather's wheelchair, perhaps to be blessed with a compliment. After all, grandpa *had* paid for all those violin lessons.

"Son, you got one hell of a nerve dragging me out here like this, you hear? Keep that damned cat-screeching fiddle at home. Some of these people think I'm actually related to you."

- - - - - - - - - - - - - - - - - - - -

"So tell me, Mr. Clemson, what can I do for you today?" I asked again.

"Yup, your old man and me...we sure had some good times. But lately, I've been spending some time at Resorts, the casino down the shore. Ever been there?"

"Can't say that I have."

"They sure know how to treat you right. I only play the quarter slots, but they know I'm a regular, so they give me the royal treatment. I get two drinks and a complimentary pass to the buffet, and I don't have to clean up afterwards. That's the part I love. Somebody else cleans up after me. Ever been there?"

"I don't believe so."

"Well I'm 78 next month, so I figured it's time I get my will wrote up."

"That's a good idea."

"I don't have no family or nothin', and my music friends are dying off. Alls that's left is Benny the piano player, Elwood the clarinetist, Sandy the cello guy, and Pat with the viola. So I want that my estate is split in fours, and each of my buddies gets one of the fours. Make Elwood the executor - he was always the bossy one."

I started to take notes as my client rambled on.

"Now here's the special part. I had really fond memories of your fadder, but he's gone. Nowadays I got a warm spot in my heart for the folks at Resorts, 'cause they treat me so good. So I've decided I want to be cremated. But I want my ashes spread *inside* the casino. I want to hear them quarter slot bells for all eternity."

I stopped taking notes.

"I beg your pardon?"

"You got to write it in the will just like I said. I don't want my ashes spread on a beach or tossed out of some plane. That's stupid. No. I want mine put in the casino where I can still be part of the action. Just make sure the janitors don't sweep me up and throw me away. I was a janitor for forty-five years. And let me tell you, them Resort guys are damn thorough."

"Mr. Clemson..."

"Look Larry, don't give me none of that lawyer we-got-a-problem-here crap. I was your fadder's best friend. So I want you to treat me like Resorts, where the customer is always right. Just go ahead and put it in the will like I'm tellin' you."

And so I did.

- - - - - - - - - - - - - - - - - - -

"There's a Mr. Sakaschitz, Elwood Sakaschitz, here to see you," my receptionist reported.

"Does he have an appointment?" I asked.

"He says it'll just take a minute."

I made my way over to the waiting room. Some guy with grey hair molded in the shape of a horseshoe affixed to the back of his head stood by the window.

"Fox?"

"Yes?"

"Elwood Sakaschitz - clarinetist. Well, I guess you heard..."

"...Forgive me, heard what?"

"Clemy died Tuesday. You wrote his will last year, right?"

"Who is? ... Wait ... Yes! Clemy. The violin guy!"

"Yeah. Your dad's best friend. He died Tuesday."

"I'm so sorry to hear that."

"During my last visit to the hospital he told me about some special instructions that you drafted regarding his ashes. Is that true? The funeral director needs to know."

"Special instructions?"

"Resorts. He wants to spend eternity at Resorts."

"I'm afraid I don't recall...Oh my God!"

"Yup. I guess you do now. By the way, you're supposed to handle the estate - another one of Clemy's dying wishes. He trusted you to follow his instructions about his ashes."

"Yeah, but you can't be serious about dumping his cremains in - "

"Fox, you wouldn't deny Clemy his last dying wish? Even an executioner has enough compassion to give a condemned man his final cigarette."

Guilt. The one motivating factor stronger than a woman's tears. I could see a bus ride to Atlantic City in my near future. Elwood sensed that he had presented a persuasive argument.

"Good. I'm glad that's settled. Don't worry about a thing. Clemy thought of every detail. He wrote his instructions right here."

The clarinetist produced a worn notepad hidden in his shirt pocket, and waved the codicil at me. "Ever been to the Atlantic City casinos?"

"Can't say that I have. By the way, who's coming with us?"

"There's Benny. He's the piano player, so he's not very bright. On the other hand, we can count on him to improvise if necessary. He's been playing accompaniment so long he follows directions without putting up much fuss. Pat will tag along. He's a violist, so you'll hardly know he's there. Sandy, the cellist is strung a little tight, but aren't we all in our own way? And you and me. That makes the entire quintet."

The next Sunday, we met at the downtown bus depot along with what appeared to be 40 or 50 retirees eager to part with their hard-earned wages. There was electricity in the air as those who anticipated amassing small fortunes with the crank of a handle or the turn of a wheel began to swap lies of prior conquests. Apparently, no one in this crowd had ever lost a penny.

"And then this old biddy from Conshohocken gets up from her machine after only two hours of feeding it nickels, so she can go to the lav. Well, I plop down, drop in just two coins, and hit for $38.00! That's the most expensive dump she'll ever take!"

Everyone gasped as the ancient storyteller shook his head up and down in silent confirmation, similar to an Atlantic City headliner acknowledging his admiring audience.

Three hours and a free roll of quarters later, we arrived at Resorts Casino. I hadn't seen so much confusion since my days as a laborer at the steel plant. There was money dropping out of machines, money being dropped into machines, lights blinking, bells ringing and people screaming. I felt as if I had entered the third plateau of Dante's Inferno.

"Outta my way," the ancient storyteller announced from behind us. There was no time to lose - just nickels and dimes.

Elwood turned to his fellow conspirators. "Gentlemen," he announced solemnly, "let us proceed."

He walked unhesitatingly to a large potted rubber plant standing against a back wall. It was thriving within the jungle of half dollar slot machines. We had entered the world of high rollers. Our fearless guide produced his little notebook and studied it momentarily.

"O.K. Now everyone form a semi-circle with your back to the rubber plant."

Compliant Benny did as he was told. Emotional Pat started to cry, but moved into position, too. Sandy took a giant step backward.

"What are we doing here?" I asked Sakaschitz.

"Placing Clemy in his eternal resting place."

"Where?"

"Under the rubber plant. Now close ranks."

"Under the what?"

"Look, Fox, there's security cameras focused in on every slot machine and toilet seat in this joint - not on the vegetation. Now on my count, we're going to feel behind us, gently lift the plant a few inches, then I'll toss Ol' Clemy in the pot. In a month's time, they'll be watering his stem and polishing his leaves."

It was then that Elwood stunned us all by producing a large clear zip-lock bag filled with gray dust and white grain. He studied the contents for a moment.

"Good-bye, Clemy," he said somberly.

"I won! I won!" some giddy gambler screamed two aisles away.

I instinctively found my designated spot next to the rubber plant. One or two leaves poked my neck.

"On the count of three, gentlemen," Elwood directed. It was as if we were about to play a quintet.

"Ah-one and ah-two and ah-three..."

I reached behind me while standing shoulder-to-shoulder with these musicians. These friends. We yanked the unsuspecting plant out of its protective pot. Then I heard the sound of sand being poured to its destiny. We inched the plant back into its ornamental brass container. Clemy's last request had been honored.

That afternoon I ate at the Gamblers' Buffet. I never had better hot pastrami. The lady next to me claimed she had just won $64. Clemy was probably watching when she struck it rich.

Chapter 4
The Customer Is Always Right

CHAPTER 5

WHAT COMES AROUND GOES AROUND

Cleveland Benjamin needed some money, so he went to the First National Bank and robbed it at gunpoint. The assistant manager gave him a satchel of cash with exploding dye. When Cleveland exited the bank, he decided to do an impromptu inventory of his newfound wealth. Upon opening the booby-trapped pouch, the unexpected on-rush of red spray rendered him nauseated, temporarily blind, and immobile. The cops found him sitting on the front bank steps, surrounded by 47 loose one-dollar bills, all of them newly coated with incriminating red dye.

I was assigned as Cleveland's free public defender because Cleveland claimed he was indigent. That was true. The police had confiscated Cleveland's only $47 as evidence.

Cleveland peered at me from between the bars of his jail cell. "I'm innocent," he proclaimed. "And you better get me off." Minutes later, he was ushered to the prison infirmary to start the long process of scrubbing the red dye off his face and hands.

The trial took two days to complete. Judge "if-you-waste-my-time-with-a-useless-trial-I'll-sentence-you-to-20-years-on-the-license-plate-middle-shift-assembly-line" Clinton Budd Palmer presided. The district attorney ran the bank videotape showing Cleveland entering the lobby with a drawn gun.

"Do you plan to present any type of defense?" I whispered in my client's ear.

"I thought that was *your* job, idiot! You better get me off," he reminded me.

The district attorney put the assistant manager on the witness stand.

"Yes," she confirmed as she pointed with dramatic flair toward Cleveland. "That's the bank robber who stole the money. He was only three feet away. I'll never forget his ugly face."

I looked at Cleveland. "Is there anything in particular you'd like me to ask her?" My client turned his ugly face toward me.

"You better get me off," he reminded me. "Twenty years of license plates is not how I plan to spend my golden years."

The district attorney called the arresting officer to testify. The cop motioned at Cleveland.

"Yeah, that's the guy we found with the marked money and.red dye on his face."

Cleveland glared at me.

"I know, I know," I repeated. "I better get you off."

The jury deliberated for 15 minutes. Then they found my client guilty as charged. Judge Palmer sentenced Cleveland to 20 years, which I thought was rather lenient given the facts of the case.

Cleveland didn't share my viewpoint. So he petitioned the county to provide him with a new free attorney who would be charged with the task of suing me, predicated upon the claim that Cleveland had failed to receive a fair trial because he had been represented by ineffective counsel. That, arguably, was true. My presence at trial had had little or no impact on anything.

Cleveland raised a second rather creative issue, never before considered by the court. He claimed that he had, during his pre-trial incarceration, asked the warden to grant him personal access to the county courthouse law library, so that he might better prepare for trial. The warden had declined this request.

"I was discriminated against," Cleveland wrote in his federal civil lawsuit, "just because I was indigent."

"If I could have posted bail," he continued, "I would have visited the law library to prepare my own defense."

With extra time on his hands Cleveland worked diligently on his lawsuit. He named as defendants the County of Northampton, its warden, the county executive, all of the county council members, the district attorney, and me. He asked for more than $1 million in damages.

Each year the county and its representatives are named in dozens of lawsuits, so Cleveland's complaint was sent to the county's insurance carrier - the same carrier that processed claims dealing with county motor vehicle accidents, and slip-and-fall cases on county land. Cleveland's case landed on the desk of some associate in a 300-lawyer firm in downtown Philadelphia - the firm that handled all the insurance carrier's claims.

The insurance company and the Philadelphia lawyer reviewed Cleveland's file, and concluded that it would cost more than $50,000 in legal fees to defend the matter in Federal Court where, theoretically, a "runaway" jury might award poor Cleveland a million dollars or more. Or the county could settle out of court. So they offered Cleveland $5,000 and threw in a county library card, so he could take out up to five books a week for delivery to his prison quarters.

"Five Thousand Dollars!" Cleveland exclaimed from the depths of his jail cell as he read the insurance company's certified letter. That was more money than Cleveland had amassed during his last three armed robberies.

"I've been in the wrong business," he mumbled.
He took the deal.

The insurance carrier and its Philadelphia lawyer did not see the need to advise any of us defendants of the settlement. After all, if the Philadelphia lawyer had written a separate letter of explanation to the warden, the county executive, the seven members of county council, the district attorney and me, it would have cost another $628 in legal fees. And that's *exactly* what the insurance company was trying to avoid.

About a week later, President Judge Clinton Budd Palmer was having his usual first cup of coffee in chambers. He reached for the morning newspaper. The front-page headline caught his attention.

County pays inmate $5,000 over library dispute.

The judge's clerk quickly summoned a janitor to help clean up the coffee his honor had involuntarily projected onto the desk in front of him. The judge eventually recovered from the shaking hands and twitching eyes, but his face was still bright red.

"Get the Benjamin file," he bellowed, "and find out when he's next scheduled to appear before me!"

His Honor didn't have long to wait. The federal case concerning library usage might have been settled, but Benjamin's criminal appeal, based upon my incompetence at time of his jury trial, was still pending. Just two weeks after the coffee spray hit the desk, we all gathered in Courtroom Number One to address Mr. Benjamin's claim that I hadn't adequately represented him.

There was Cleveland, the proud possessor of a county library card, dressed in an orange prison jumpsuit with matching leg and ankle shackles. Standing next to him was Herbie Hancock, Cleveland's newest "free" attorney, paid for by the county taxpayers. Previously, at time of the trial, I was the district attorney's adversary. Now I sat with him as his primary witness to testify that I was truly brilliant and competent as Cleveland Benjamin's prior legal counsel.

"Before we proceed with this morning's hearing, I have a question or two," the learned judge mused from his imposing bench. "Are you the same Cleveland Benjamin who recently was paid $5,000 by the county's insurance carrier?"

Benjamin hesitated to answer. After all, what did his financial status have to do with his claim that I was incompetent?

His Honor didn't bother to wait for an answer. He simply dangled a white piece of paper from his left hand. "You see, Mr. Benjamin, you signed this form when you applied for free legal counsel. You swore in paragraph one that you were indigent. You swore in paragraph two that if your status were to change, you would immediately advise the court and obtain private counsel. Did you do that, Mr. Benjamin?"

The prisoner was starting to get the same bad feeling as when he opened the booby-trapped moneybag. For the first time in his life, he was a man of some means. He had even begun to plan a little catered affair at the prison for some of his closest incarcerated friends. The judge's questions began to cast some doubt on whether this highly anticipated social event would now take place.

"Wait a minute," the felon stammered. "That ain't fair." He looked at his newest incompetent attorney, Herbie Hancock. "Do something, you idiot. Don't just stand there!"

There was little Attorney Hancock could do.

"You are dismissed as counsel in this appeal," Judge Palmer advised Hancock. "As for you, Mr. Benjamin, I suggest you retain private counsel with your new found wealth." Herbie and I picked up our briefcases and left the courtroom.

Rumor has it that Cleveland tried to hire a new lawyer to prove that Hancock and I were both incompetent. Unfortunately for Benjamin, competent lawyers around here want a $10,000 retainer.

Chapter 5
What Comes Around Goes Around

CHAPTER 6

THE ART OF DANCE

I watch as a grocery store clerk replenishes the stock on his shelves. He puts a can of beans on the canned bean shelf; he stacks pickled beets next to other pickled beets. I envy him, for his life makes sense. I have been practicing law for more than 30 years. I have yet to find a single client who wants to stack beans with the beans.

Monica and Fernando Ramos were waiting in the solitude of my conference room. My secretary advised me that they came to discuss a "liquor license issue."

"It's the opportunity of a lifetime," Monica gushed, her long blond hair cascading around her model-gorgeous face.

"The Snakepit's up for sale," Fernando chimed in like a cub scout going on his first cookout. "We need to move on this before someone else grabs it. My friend says you do liquor license transfers. Is that right?"

I looked into Fernando's piercing black eyes. I guessed he was...maybe 25. Did this kid and blondie have the financial muscle to purchase an existing business?

"The Snakepit?" I blurted out.

"On the south side, at 17th and Lexington," said Monica.

Seventeenth and Lex? That block was no Garden of Eden. It was a neighborhood of condemned buildings and seedy bars.

"The owner wants to retire. He says after 35 years, he's had enough," Monica explained. "I used to work there part-time, so I got to know him. Next week, he's putting it up for sale."

"It's a gold mine!" Fernando assured me. "The guy is letting go of a gold mine!"

"The Snakepit?" I interjected again. "Isn't that a - don't they have strip - "

"Exotic dancing," Monica corrected.

Had I touched a nerve?

"We...the performers...are artists, you know," she explained. "Just like the ballet, people pay to see interpretive dance. Don't judge a lollipop, Mr. Fox, until you lick it."

Was the air conditioning on the blink again? I hate those hot flashes. Anyway, I wasn't judging, just conceptualizing what sounded like an interesting discipline. I've always been a patron of the arts. I've always believed in keeping an open mind. And free expression in any form has always been a cornerstone of our democracy and the American Way. A field trip to the Snakepit surely would be, if nothing else, enlightening.

"So what do we gotta do to buy the business?" Fernando naïvely questioned.

I outlined the process, from Agreement of Sale to transfer of the liquor license. "You'll probably need approvals from the city zoning hearing board, too," I theorized.

"Zoning?" Monica repeated. "The place has been there forever. Why would zoning be an issue?"

"The transfer of ownership of an 'adult use' requires special exception approval. That way, the city building and fire inspectors can perform a construction code update, to see if there's compliance with recently passed zoning and safety amendments. You might need a refurbished fire escape, or more on-site parking, or a planting buffer."

"What's all this gonna cost in legal fees?" Fernando wondered.

I told him. He didn't flinch. The young entrepreneur wrote out a check and handed it to me.

"Now you're working for us," he confirmed. "Do whatever you got to do to make this deal happen." He sounded as serious as an IRS audit notice.

"Who do I contact?"

"Amos Krazaluski. He owns the joint. I'll tell him to expect your call. Get him to sign the Agreement of Sale, so he can't sell the Snakepit to nobody else."

"We're counting on you," Monica added as she flipped her hair and blew me a kiss.

- - - - - - - - - - - - - - - - - - -

"I've been expecting your call. Come on over," Amos confirmed over the phone. "We're here 7 to 1 every night, except Sundays."

I was glad to hear the dancers were given time off to worship.

"May I come by tonight to discuss the Agreement of Sale?"

"Sure, sure. There's always room for one more."

The Snakepit sounded like an informal, friendly place, so I decided to leave my dress coat and tie at the office. However, on the off chance that I might bump into someone I knew, or who might claim to recognize me, I decided to wear my oversized Boston Red Sox baseball cap, the one that slid down over my eyebrows. And since it was a crisp March night, I also donned my nondescript blue gardening jacket with the collar that hid most of my neck and chin. I glanced in the mirror. I was unrecognizable. I drove to 17th and Lex.

Surprisingly there was no valet parking. So I parked next to an abandoned Buick resting on cinder blocks. At the entrance, I could feel the pounding beat of dance music. I pulled my cap down to the bridge of my nose, stretched my coat collar up past my mouth, took a breath, and stepped into another world.

The toothless seven-foot bouncer asked for six bucks. It was a bargain, since I would have given him my wallet had he so directed.

"Enjoy yourself," he grunted.

I made my way through a wall of exhaled smoke to the combination bar and dance area.

The circular bar had a three-foot runway, upon which a young lady had just appeared. She had made her grand entrance by sliding down a brass pole at center stage. With my head down, I looked up. Were others yet to follow?

Smoke was everywhere. I inched toward the bar and found a lopsided stool with duct-taped upholstery. Seven other patrons of the arts were similarly perched, surrounding a bartender who had the best seat in the house. I looked around. I felt at home. Each guy wore an oversized baseball cap with upturned coat collar. We were kindred spirits.

An unseen master of ceremonies began to holler into the defective speaker system.

"Gentlemen, put your hands together for our next lovely lady...Daisy!"

Three of the drunks weren't, at that moment, grasping beer bottles. They politely applauded, as did I. Daisy began her routine. She was dressed as a nurse, with crisp hospital cap, white blouse, dangling stethoscope, and matching dress that stopped 15 inches above her knees.

"Don't you wish every hospital had one of them?" the drunk slouched next to me observed.

It was a question with but one answer.

"Yes," I said.

The drunk took a gulp of beer and shook his head. He had found a new friend.

I began to suspect this performer wasn't actually a nurse. The nurses I've known have, for the most part, kept their uniforms on while working. Every time she removed a portion of her clothing, one or more of the bums would issue forth an inebriated cheer.

It was possible she was now naked. It was hard to tell. The dim lights flickered, the smoke was thick, and she didn't stand still for long. She had begun to shinny up the same pole in the opposite direction from whence she had initially arrived. Then she wrapped one finely sculptured leg sporting the tattoo of a butterfly on one ankle around the pole, and released her hands, her torso pointing downward as she hung like a fruit bat in a cave.

"Ain't she something, Larry," some other idiot to my right theorized.

My God! The clandestine figure sitting next to me knew my name! I prayed this bum called everyone "Larry."

"You're new here, counsellor. This your first trip to dreamland?"

I had been discovered. My reputation was toast.

"I'm...I'm here on behalf of a client," I insisted. "By the way, who the hell are you?"

"Your insurance agent, Joe Smithers," he laughed. "Hey, anyway, that's a good one. Got to remember that line. And I'm here to check out the building for...insurance purposes. Yeah, you lawyers sure think fast on your feet."

I wanted to assure Joe I was sincere, but at that moment, naked Daisy began slithering down the pole. Joe tossed a crumpled one-dollar bill at the wriggling figure. I could have sworn the portrait of Washington was smiling as the currency found its mark. Joe was a perfect shot.

"Ain't you gonna tip the lady?" Joe asked. "Listen, if my wife hung from a pole naked, I wouldn't be here, and Doris would be a dollar richer." Joe tossed another greenback.

The scope and depth of the talent displayed that night cannot be overstated. Health professionals weren't the only vocation represented. There was a lion tamer, a waitress or two, a railroad conductor, and a vacuum cleaner saleslady. One beauty could make the tassels glued to her breasts swirl in different directions simultaneously. One dancer jumped into the air and landed in a perfect split - a maneuver aptly named. The contortionist was most interesting, however. She picked up a dollar bill from the bar without using her hands, toes, or teeth.

"Who would've thought it possible?" the barfly next to me exclaimed as he shook his head in amazement.

Then I felt a tap on the shoulder. "You Fox?"

I swung around. "Yes..."

"Amos. Amos Krazaluski is the name. I've been expecting you. Enjoyin' the show?"

Just then a naked policewoman swung right past me hanging from a small trapeze.

"Yes," I confirmed.

"Well, what can I do for you, counsellor?"

The policewoman swung by in the other direction. Concentrate! I needed to concentrate!

"My clients would like to buy your (swing, pause) establishment. Is it for sale?"

"I suppose so," Amos lamented. "Nothing lasts forever."

The policewoman must have heard that remark. She unexpectedly slipped off her trapeze and fell on her head. Two beer guzzlers applauded.

As if by magic, an airline flight attendant, probably on layover, flew down the poll. This would be her 10 minutes of glory. The policewoman stumbled to scoop up several crumpled one-dollar bills and disappeared stage left into the shadows.

I decided to ask a few lawyerlike questions.

"How many entertainers work here, Mr. Krazaluski?"

"Just call me Kraz. Everybody calls me Kraz."

"Tell me, Kraz, how many dancers work here?"

"Usually eight on a shift. It's important to keep the right mix."

"Mix?"

"You got to diversify. I try to have a gorgeous one, an ugly one, a tall one, a slender one, one with a couple extra pounds, representatives of the major racial groups, and a genuine blonde and redhead. Around here, the clientele can tell if the color comes out of a bottle."

"Why an ugly girl?"

"Shows what you know, counselor. The girls who look like they got hit across the face with a bag of nickels always pull in the most tips."

"How can that be?"

"Look around you, Ace. The guys who come in here are losers, and they know it. No pretty dame is gonna give them the time of day. So they invest their money where it does the most good - with girls who might actually give 'em a second look."

"How much do you pay the dancers?"

"Pay? Where you from, Mars? They're all independent contractors. I get 10% of the tips. Then I pay the bartender and bouncer."

"Where do you *find* these ladies?"

"They find me. I got a waiting list. Most are students at the local colleges, hoping to put a dent in tuition. The lion tamer just got accepted to med school. The policewoman is gonna be a CPA. The nurse is studying to be a microbiologist."

Kraz told all. He explained the psychological necessity of inadequate lighting, why bouncers should not wear glasses, how to tastefully decorate the bar for the holidays, and why the menu did not have to expand beyond the sale of hot dogs and beer, hamburgers and beer, and pizza and beer.

Then we discussed minor issues such as the sales price, transfer of the liquor license, and mortgage financing. A week later, my clients had a signed Agreement of Sale, contingent upon procurement of zoning approval from the city authorities. If I won the zoning hearing, the girls would soon be gyrating for new owners, and Kraz would begin his well-deserved retirement. After all, similar to a coroner, how many naked bodies is enough?

- - - - - - - - - - - - - - - - - - -

The zoning hearing was publicly advertised, as required by law. Property owners surrounding the bar within a 500-foot radius received personal invitations to attend. A notice was also circulated in the newspaper and posted on the exterior bar room window:

Notice is given that applicants Monica and Fernando Ramos seek to conduct an adult use upon premises known as 1701 Lexington Avenue, City of Bethlehem, and Commonwealth of Pennsylvania, to wit: the operation of a bar and grill wherein nude dancing for the entertainment of patrons will be provided, Monday through Saturday, 8:00 P.M. until 2:00 A.M. Those individuals seeking to present public comment are encouraged to attend the hearing at City Hall, September 28, at 7:00 P.M.

That's the problem with a democracy. It gives people the opportunity to express their opinions, even if they don't have anything to say. And all of them decided to show up at the hearing.

I stared in disbelief as concerned citizens entered City Hall chambers. There were only two zoning hearings on the agenda, and yet every seat in the rotunda was now occupied. Sure, there was a guy who needed a four-foot side yard setback to construct a patio in his backyard. But these folks, some dressed in clerical garb, weren't here for that.

"Do you think they are here about the nude dancing?" Fernando whispered in my ear.

The first hearing, which took less than two minutes, ended with the five zoning hearing board members granting permission to build the patio.

"Next is the application of Monica and Fernando Ramos to permit nude dancing in a bar and grill," the zoning administrator announced. A collective gasp escaped from the citizen spectators.

"Are the applicants present?"

I slowly stood up with my clients, and approached the zoning hearing board. I wasn't exactly bathed in confidence as we moved down to the front table.

"There they are!" someone behind me called out. "The perverts!"

Angry murmurs of similar sentiment rippled forward.

"You may present your case," the chairperson proclaimed.

My clients testified that nude dancing had been the featured entertainment at the Snakepit for more than 30 years, and that they wished to continue this artistic tradition. I then explained that the Supreme Court of Pennsylvania had recently confirmed that nude dancing is a form of constitutionally protected free speech, and is recognized as a lawful activity. The Board was unimpressed, and asked if any objectors cared to comment. The floodgates opened.

During the next two hours, my clients were compared to Bonnie and Clyde, Adolph Hitler, and Pontius Pilate. Nude dancing was equated to the atom bomb, killer bees, and Sodom and Gomorrah. One opponent, during a dramatic confrontational moment, pointed at me and yelled, "And you! You're no better, you...you...LAWYER!"

The hearing didn't end until 11:00 p.m. More than 40 irate citizens placed comments on record. The zoning hearing board decided it would need another month to deliberate, so they turned out the lights and everyone went home.

I stumbled into my house about midnight. I needed to unwind for a few minutes, so I turned on the TV. Some guy with a gun was arguing with another guy with a gun about a drug deal gone bad, so they shot each other. The camera zoomed in for an entertaining close-up of the blood and guts oozing from each man's bullet holes.

I've decided to take a vacation next month in Rome, where nudes have been admired for centuries as they've danced uninhibited on the ceilings.

Chapter 6
The Art of Dance

CHAPTER 7

DON'T CASH THAT CHECK

Witches aren't recruited or converted. They are born possessing powers that with time surface, are refined, and are then utilized. Sometimes one may not even realize he or she is a witch until *things* start happening.

It was a Thursday. I had been working late because my law office overhead check was due the next morning, and, as usual, I didn't have the money. For 30 years I've worked as a lawyer and have listened to countless clients declare that I charge too much, and that since I'm probably a millionaire, I should drastically reduce my fee. For the same 30 years, I've routinely been about a week shy of filing my own bankruptcy petition. Logically, I could charge myself a reasonable fee and make some money - similar to the two Russian peasants who were so broke, they did each other's laundry to generate income.

So I worked into the wee hours that night in the futile hope I'd generate a couple of elusive bucks and actually pay my secretary before the payroll checks bounced. Secretaries like to be paid once a week like clockwork. Clients don't often share the same inclination when it comes to compensating me, because I'm already rich.

The telephone rang. A paying client to save the day?

"Hello?" I began.

"Is this voicemail?" asked a man.

I actually thought of answering "yes" to see what would happen.

"No," I confirmed.

"Oh."

"May I help you?" I repeated.

"Is this Fox Esquire?"

Nobody but a nut would have addressed me that way. What on earth had possessed me to pick up the phone?

"Who is this?" I demanded.

"Jack...Jack Fleishman," came the friendly response, as if we had been buddies since childhood.

"Who?"

"Jack...over at the Ford dealership...Jack Fleishman. We met last year during high school graduation ceremonies. My daughter and your aunt's grandson were in the same class."

"Of course," I fumbled.

"Listen, Esquire, I'm calling with good news. Ferdie Fedorik has decided to toss his hat into the ring and enter the May primary as a candidate for judge of the Court of Common Pleas. I'm proud as punch to advise you that Ferdie has chosen me to be his campaign chairman and that we're counting on your support."

Ferdie Fedorik! Not the horse's ass appearing in the TV ad where, with a gavel in one hand and the scales of justice swinging back and forth in the other, he implores his astonished audience to lay their marital problems at his doorstep. Wasn't he the guy who advertised on the cover of the phone book, the ad with the removable sticky coupon magnet for $10 off the first office consultation?

"Ferdie's running for judge?" I gasped into the receiver.

"And he needs your help. Can I tell him you're good for a small contribution? Say $500?"

Five hundred American dollars? Was he insane? I hadn't passed "go" or collected $200 the entire week. I had to think fast. What if this guy Fleishman sensed some hesitation on my part and Fedorik actually got elected? On the other hand, this telephone call signaled the beginning of the election season. How many other lawyers would be announcing their candidacy? Proper allotment of my limited resources required careful thought.

"Jack," I began. "Can I call you back? I'm in the middle of something right now."

"You betcha," he gushed. "And thanks for being on our team."

42

Fifteen years ago when I bought my split level home, I alone had to cough up the down payment and scratch for the 12% 30 year mortgage.   Maybe I should have called Ferdie.

"Hello, who is this?"

"Larry."

"Larry? Larry who?"

"C'mon. You know who, Ferdie. It's your pal, Larry the lawyer, in Bethlehem. Remember? We rode the elevator together once at the courthouse. Listen, I'm thinking of buying a house, and I was wondering if you might help with the down payment. Can I count on you for...say...$500? Settlement is already scheduled, so I'll need your check soon."

- - - - - - - - - - - - - - - - - - - -

The problem, of course, is the unspoken, but implied threat. If I fail to make a "voluntary" donation and the candidate wins office, there's a chance every lawyer in the courtroom who sent some money will receive a fairer share of impartial Justice than will I. And so each election, I write out those stinkin' checks.

It was my CPA, Harvey Gilsap, who first pointed out the interesting correlation just three days after Fleishman's unsolicited telephone call. Gilsap and my secretary were finishing up my quarterly tax report. He emerged from her office and motioned to me.

"I just noticed something rather unusual, Larry."

"What's that, Harvey?"

"Your political contributions."

"What about them?"

"At first I thought it was just a fluke, but then I went back into your records for the last 15 years. Are you aware that not a single candidate you gave money to ever served in office?"

"You mean to tell me not one of those guys ever got elected?" I laughed.

"Not exactly," explained Harvey. "I said they never served in office."

"I don't follow."

"Over the last 15 years, there have been numerous primaries and five elections for judge. You wrote out 35 checks for 35 different campaigns."

"Thirty-five!"

"As far as I can tell, a couple of the candidates actually were elected, but they died or other problems arose before they ever got to wear their judicial robes."

"Are you sure, Harvey?"

"Here's the list. Look for yourself."

I scanned the names. If memory served, four lawyers had actually been elected, but one of them was unexpectedly disbarred, one committed suicide, one drove into a bridge abutment, and the last dropped dead - all before their swearing-in ceremonies. The thirty-one other members of the bar simply lost.

"I *must* have backed at least one winner," I gasped.

"I don't think so," my bean counter mused. "You're batting 1,000."

The next day, Jack Fleishman telephoned. "Well, Esquire, it's been almost a week. Can Ferdie Fedorik count on you? Surely you won't miss a lousy $500 bucks."

"Mr. Fleishman," I began, "I don't think you want my money."

"I beg your pardon?"

"Any time I've made a political contribution to a judicial race, the candidate has failed to take office."

I thought I heard laughing at the other end of this candid conversation.

"Good one, Esquire. No one ever handed me that excuse before. But seriously, I'd like to come by for the check today. Are you on our team or not?"

I went over to United Central Bank and put $500 more on my credit line. Then I left a check with my receptionist. An hour later, someone came by and picked it up. I figured that was the last of it.

The next afternoon I received a call from the Snydersville police department.

"Attorney Fox?"

"Yes?"

"Captain Skidmore, Snydersville Police."

"Good afternoon, Captain."

"Attorney Fox, did you write a check to the 'Committee to Elect Ferdie Fedorik Judge'?"

My heart skipped a beat. "Listen, Captain, I can explain. I transferred money from my line of credit. Sometimes it takes a day or two for the check to clear. I'll make good on the ..."

"Attorney Fox..."

"Yes?"

"I have some unsettling news. Yesterday, Mr. Fedorik entered the Merchants Trust Savings & Loan here in Snydersville. He was about to cash your check, but before he could hand it to the teller, a masked gunman entered the S & L. Fedorik, from the tapes we saw, made a sudden move to put your check back into his pocket. The robber shot him dead."

"Oh my God!"

"I just wanted you to know we're keeping the check as evidence. It will be returned after criminal proceedings are concluded."

"Thirty-six out of 36!" I stammered.

"I beg your pardon?"

"Oh, nothing Captain, nothing at all."

- - - - - - - - - - - - - - - - - - -

The primary election had begun to heat up. Four lawyers ultimately announced for one open judgeship. Among the candidates was Felix Groman. Felix was a vicious, untrustworthy, self-centered egomaniac who brought no honor to the practice of law. His ascension to the Bench would be a travesty. My telephone rang.

"Hi. This is Alphonse Filiponi."

"Who?"

"About a year ago, we met at a dance recital in Nazareth. My neighbor's granddaughter was performing."

"How can I help you?"

"I have received the rare honor of being named chairman of the 'Felix Groman For Judge' committee. I was wondering if you might..."

"Mr. Filiponi," I interrupted, "may I make a contribution to the campaign?"

"How very kind."

"My receptionist will have a check for you today."

"I will advise our next judge of your generosity."

I wrote out a check for $25 and put it in an envelope at the front desk.

Chapter 7
Don't Cash That Check

CHAPTER 8

ONE STEP AT A TIME

Angelo Berdini had been managing his blouse mill for 30 years. Once a prosperous business, it now languished. And when things got tough, he'd phone me.

"The gas company says my service will be shut off next week if I don't bring the account current. Can you call them and negotiate for smaller monthly payments?"

He employed 60 women hunched over outdated sewing machines, and each laborer demanded union wages like clockwork on Friday. Somewhere in China or Mexico, 60 other pieceworkers toiled longer hours at a mere fraction of these set wages.

When Angelo's father started the business after returning from service in World War II, there were dozens of blouse mills in the Lehigh Valley. Now just three remained. Angelo was a loyal client. He kept me on as corporate counsel after his father died. Over the years, we had become friends.

"Angelo's on the phone," my secretary announced.

She didn't have to give a second name. There was only one client named "Angelo," and he called at least once a week. Maybe OSHA was driving him nuts with some new regulation. Perhaps some bureaucrat in Harrisburg needed to justify his existence with another sales tax audit. He called, too, when the garment workers' union was threatening war.

Talking to Angelo wasn't a chore. He didn't feel sorry for himself, he never blamed anyone for his problems, and he understood that, like sewing machine operators, lawyers had to be paid.

"Hi, Angelo. How's it going?"

"I just received a new order for thermal shirts, so the lights will be on at least another two weeks," he quipped.

"Here's the thing," Angelo began. "Last week the wife and I went over to the grocery store on Center Street

48

'cause they had liverwurst on special. As we were leaving the store, I missed this one step down near the curb, and I tripped and fell. I broke my right baby toe."

"Did you see the step before you fell?"

"I don't recall. It happened so fast. One second I was up. The next, I was sprawled on the parking lot."

"Did you go to the doctor?"

"Yup. He put a bandage around my toe, and told me to stay off my feet for two days. Two days of no supervision at the mill! When I returned to work, sleeves were sewn on backwards, collars were cut incorrectly, and some buttonholes were missing buttons. Can I be compensated for the two days? I lost a couple of bucks."

"How much?"

"I don't know exactly. Maybe one or two thousand. I had to reattach 70 collars and half a day's worth of sleeves.

"Are you O.K. now?"

"I guess so. I went back to work, and the pain has subsided."

Angelo's little mishap did not sound, at first blush, like the stuff from which substantial jury verdicts are derived. Had this been some stranger calling out of the blue, I would have declined to pursue the conversation.

"Angelo..."

"Yes?"

"The costs of a trial might exceed any verdict awarded," I offered diplomatically.

"My toe is still black and blue," the victim interjected.

"I doubt the grocery store's insurance company will make much of an offer, other than to reimburse you personally for two days' lost wages."

"But I had pain and suffering - as well as shirt sleeves to fix. If it was the toe of the president of the insurance company, I bet he'd make himself an offer to settle the case before he had to sue himself!"

It was hard to argue with such logic, even though this case had little value, if any. Just because Angelo tripped on a step didn't necessarily mean the grocery store was responsible for buttonless shirts. If I placed a call or two with some insurance investigator, or if I had to write some letters, my legal fee would easily exceed the entire pittance offered for nuisance value. I explained all of this to Angelo.

"I still want you to sue. The store owners broke my toe by luring me to their doorstep with cheap liverwurst."

Angelo was my friend. His toe was broken. Some of his sleeves were on backwards. Some of his buttonholes weren't holes at all. I couldn't abandon him in his hour of need.

I wrote a letter of representation to the grocery store conglomerate - a national business entity with 20 full-time lawyers on retainer. My letter was referred to a corporate subsidiary that self-insured all 348 grocery stores in the United States, Canada, Puerto Rico, and the Virgin Islands. One week later I received a response from the computer in its Philadelphia district office.

> *Dear Sir:*
> *Your   claim   #A32-Z196   received.*
> *Investigation completed. Corporation not liable. No damages found.*
>
> *Look for more buy-one-get-one specials each time you shop.*
>
> *Very truly yours,*
>
> *Office of Claims Adjustment*

No signature. I sent a copy to Angelo.

"I still want to sue," he confirmed.

I drafted a formal complaint in which pleading I outlined the chronology of events leading up to my client's unfortunate injury. I described the damages sustained. I had Angelo review the allegations before I filed the document with the Clerk of Courts.

"You forgot to tell 'em my toe turned black and blue," he corrected.

I added that assertion. Then I took the formal pleading to the courthouse, and "clocked" it in, advancing a filing fee of $150. I had the Sheriff of Northampton County serve the complaint on a representative of the grocery store conglomerate, at a further expenditure of $125. I had spent four hours drafting the complaint. Costs and fees now exceeded any possible settlement offer.

It had been a month since Angelo had fallen. He decided to call me.

"What's taking so long? Did they make an offer yet?"

Two weeks later, I got a phone call from a lawyer whose name didn't sound familiar.

"It's Attorney Thurgood Rodfong," my secretary announced.

"Who?"

"Says he got your black-and-blue toe complaint."

"Huh? My what?"

I made the mistake of picking up the phone.

"Hello?"

"You Fox?"

(I am *such* a fox, but how did he know?)

"Yes," I confirmed as I continued to sift through three other pressing files on my desk.

"Got your complaint about the broken baby toe..." Rodfong paused. "Do you know why our grocery stores probably won't be able to continue liverwurst at a special price? 'Cause of blood-sucking ambulance-chasers like you, pumping out nuisance value complaints by the basket load!"

"Nice to make your acquaintance," I interjected.

Rodfong was on a roll. There was no stopping this freight train.

"See, there isn't any free lunch. When a bottom-feeder like you files a frivolous complaint like this, it places a burden on our entire system of jurisprudence, and then the price of liverwurst goes up."

"Does that mean you're not inclined to tender an offer to settle the case out of court?"

"Listen, Buster..."

"It's 'Fox'..."

"Whatever. If your client was dying of thirst in the Sahara Desert, I wouldn't give him the sweat off my left - "

That's when I hung up. Next stop? Formal baby toe litigation.

I told Angelo about my discussion with Rodfong.

"What happens next?"

"You'll be deposed."

"Will it hurt?"

"No, Angelo. It means the attorney for the grocery store will ask you questions under oath about your accident, and how it affected shirt production. A stenographer will take down what you say. The transcript can be used at time of trial."

Rodfong proved to be even more belligerent in person. He had a permanent sneer painted on his pugnacious face. He swaggered before us, his clenched fists deposited in the pockets of his oversized pants held by oversized suspenders. He weighed in at a cool 280 - easily - but it was all flab. He was the type of adversary who thrived on his ability to make everyone in a room ill-at-ease. In a word, he was worth every penny the grocery conglomerate was paying him.

"What do you mean you didn't see the step down?" he barked in Angelo's face. "Did you ever shop there before? When? How many times a week do you usually trip over yourself? How many frivolous complaints have you filed?"

"Objection!" I shouted.

Rodfong chuckled as his pudgy hands shuffled the piles of documents positioned before him.

- - - - - - - - - - - - - - - - - - -

I was as ready for trial as I'd ever be. Angelo wanted his day in court, and the jury sat in anticipation before us. Rodfong, in a blatant attempt to look human, tried to smile at the jury from his seat at the defense table. Then he stared at old Judge Manfred Krempasky. His Honor had recently announced he was retiring from the bench, perhaps as early as next month. This insanity might well be his last jury trial.

I put my client on the stand. He testified that he tripped and fell, breaking his baby toe. As a result, he was out of work for two days. Rodfong struggled to lift himself out of his chair, and then approached Angelo to commence his grilling cross-examination.

He and his menacing attitude stood 10 feet in front of the witness stand. Rodfong, true to form, shoved his clenched fat fists into his pants pockets, placing obvious strain on his Brooks Brothers suspenders.

But it was something else that had suddenly caught the jury's eye. As it so happened, defense counsel, when last faced with the task, had failed to zip his pants. The stress of his fists pressing into his pockets had caused the zipper opening to widen substantially, thereby exposing his red heart boxers and their printed embellishment, "Who's Your Daddy?" And, so, for the first time, it appeared that swaggering Rodfong might actually have a softer side, so to speak.

Never before had I seen a jury so focused. Twenty-four eyes followed counsel's every move. It wasn't until the judge called for redirect that his honor noticed Rodfong's wardrobe faux pas, as well, and with haste, called a recess.

"We'll take a five-minute break, Ladies and Gentlemen," the judge announced as the tipstaff called out *all rise*. Everyone stood up as His Honor made his way from the bench, past Angelo still perched in the witness box. Judge Krempasky felt embarrassed for poor Rodfong, and wished to exit the courtroom quickly. Unfortunately, he failed to negotiate the one step that gave his bench its lofty position. He tripped and fell, crying out in pain as he remained sprawled on the courtroom floor. The tipstaff ran to his aid as the horrified jurors looked on.

"I think I broke my damn toe," the judge gasped, as he clutched his ankle. "That one lousy step!"

They carried Judge Krempasky out on a stretcher. I glanced knowingly at a flustered Rodfong and his protruding underwear.

"I'll give you $10,000 to settle," he mumbled.

"I'll run it by my client," I replied.

Chapter 8
One Step At a Time

CHAPTER 9

THE LEGAL FEE

It had been an unusual divorce proceeding from the start. Neither one possessed the financial resources to leave the house, and so he hid in his bedroom and she slept in hers. The small pre-fabricated one-story dwelling had just one outdated bathroom, so he showered in the morning - if he got out of bed - and she claimed sole possession of the plumbing fixtures in the evening.

Angry Fern and indifferent Reginald had been married for 37 years, and they got their money's worth, because it felt much longer. They bought their house on its undersized lot right after their honeymoon in Newark, N. J. Then, with time, the new house and their marriage began to disintegrate without any attempt to repair either one. Two years earlier he had retired as a laborer in the cement company-bagging department, the only place on the face of the earth where he had found happiness and a sense of purpose to his otherwise mundane life.

He started moping around the house. He'd drink his first beer about 11:00 in the morning, while reclining in the basement recreation room. Around midnight, the TV flickered light on his limp body. His last beer of the day sat warm and fizzless on the end table. He had no other diversions or friends. They were still sweating over at the cement company.

They had no children, since that would have required some intimacy. She had worked for a while at the corner discount store. Then it went out of business, so she stayed home, and took up complaining about him on a full-time basis. At first she had thought he might be a "fixer-upper," but her helpful criticisms never resulted in any noticeable improvement. Thirty-seven years of marriage, and he still didn't know there was a hamper in the house.

"I want a divorce," she proclaimed from the other side of my conference room table. These were not the words of a woman undecided.

"There's more to life than watching somebody drink a case of beer each day. I never knew so much booze could go in one end and out the other."

"Has your husband retained an attorney?" I inquired.

"Doubt it. He don't care what I do."

Fern wasn't much of a talker. Her tired eyes and unkempt gray hair gave witness to the fact that she hadn't experienced a happy moment in some time. I wondered when last she had forced a smile. Did she remember how to smile? Had she ever been in love?

"What's this gonna cost me? He won't agree to nothin'. Hell, he won't even talk about it."

Actually, the pursuit of a divorce is a study in arithmetic and fractions: Who will get how much of the marital pie. I explained that she was entitled to a percentage of Reginald's pension plan, and that other assets acquired during the marriage would be subject to equitable distribution.

"Do you feel physically threatened by your husband's presence in the house?"

The question seemed to take Fern by surprise. She stopped staring down at the table, and looked at me.

"If he ever raised a hand, it'd mean he actually cared about something. Anything."

I filed a complaint in divorce on behalf of my newest client. Reginald didn't respond. He didn't hire an attorney, either. He ignored my letters seeking to schedule a meeting. Weeks dragged into months. The couple continued to sleep in separate rooms in separate worlds.

"Can't you do something?" Fern whined over the phone.

I explained that we could unilaterally schedule a hearing before the Master in divorce, the hearing officer assigned to adjudicate this dispute, and this might prompt Reginald to start taking legal proceedings seriously.

"How much will it cost?" asked Fern.

I told her. Silence.

"Why so much?" she finally gasped.

"The master requires payment in full in advance. Otherwise, he won't schedule a hearing - a hearing that could take as long as a week."

"But that's an insane amount of money."

"Well, that includes my legal fees to attend the hearing. As I advised you in my initial fee agreement letter, I charge by the hour. That's why I've tried for the better part of a year to convince you to come to an amicable settlement with your husband. You can literally save thousands of dollars in hearing costs."

"I just want to get rid of my husband! How long could it possibly take?"

"I have to prepare for what may be a complex and protracted trial. There will be dozens of exhibits and testimony to prepare, including reports from an accountant and an appraiser. Easily over 50 hours of trial preparation may be necessitated."

Again, silence.

"Fine. Do it. Schedule the damn hearing. I don't care what it takes. I'm not staying in this living hell no more. I'll send a check."

And she did. The master set a hearing date, and I sent Reginald formal notice - an act that seemed unnecessary - since Fern could have yelled the information through his bedroom door. He didn't respond, even though my letter advised him he could possibly lose his wife and a good deal of his assets.

As the hearing date approached, I geared up for the inevitable confrontation. The accountant we hired drafted actuarial tables depicting the value of the cement company pension plan both in present and future dollar computations. The real estate appraiser gave her best guess regarding the price an imaginary willing buyer might pay for the run-down residence. I obtained the blue book value for the family car. With just three days to go until the Wednesday morning hearing, I confirmed with a stenographer that she would be available to record the proceedings.

I worked late Tuesday night to put the finishing touches on some of the next day's exhibits. That's when the phone rang. Who'd be calling this late?

"It's Fern."

Who the hell was...Oh...*that* Fern! "Hi, Fern. Are you ready for tomorrow?"

"Listen, how much stuff have you done up to this point?"

"I beg your pardon?"

"You know, them papers or whatever for the Mister."

"The Master. I've worked on your file most of the week. I'm ready to proceed tomorrow as scheduled."

"Well, I think our little dispute here has finally been resolved, so I figured the first person I ought to call is you. Stop the meter from spinning, O.K.? And don't do any more lawyering or charge any more fees."

"I'm pleased to hear that you've come to a compromise. I assure you, I never look forward to these unpleasant proceedings. Actually, many couples, when confronted with a master's hearing, finally come to a last minute resolution. It's not that unusual. Does it appear that your husband will voluntarily leave the house?"

"Sorta. But you an' me - we have an agreement that the legal fees stop right here and now. Right?"

"Yes, Fern, unless you require that I draft a formal document outlining how things are to be divided."

"Nope. Not necessary. Do I get some of my money back?"

"Yes, you do. For one thing, most of the Master's fee will be returned. Furthermore, I appreciate the timeliness of your call," I said. "Now I can go home, and this frees up the rest of my week."

"Yeah, great for you...whatever..." she noted. "Hey, I got one more question."

"Go ahead."

"Are we off the meter?"

"We're off."

"Well, a little while ago, I walked by Reggie's room and his door was open a crack. Curiosity got the better of me, so I peeked in. Guess what?"

"I can't imagine."

"He hung himself. I called you first so you'd stop the meter."

"Oh my God! Is there anything I can do?"

"Not really. Should I cut him down or just call the cops? Oh! Before I forget, exactly how much of a refund will you be sending me?"

Chapter 9
The Legal Fee

CHAPTER 10

DON'T FORGET THE PIANO BENCH

When an elderly person dies, it's not uncommon to see just a few mourners at the funeral. The decedent has simply outlived most of his close friends and associates. The few survivors present rarely reflect the multitude of individuals whose lives were touched by the dearly departed.

Happily, such was not the case with Elmo Lillycrap. His passing at the age of 97 was acknowledged by both an overflow crowd at the evening viewing, and at the next morning's church service. The outpouring of love by the community wasn't surprising. Even after Elmo's beloved wife of 60 years had gone on to her reward, Elmo, a deeply religious man, never lost heart. Rather, he continued to tend to the needs of the less fortunate at his retirement home. He prayed with those broken in spirit and comforted them in their hour of need, and his sincere and unselfish efforts to grace others with kindness was remarkable.

It had been my privilege to know Elmo, his wife Doris, and their two sons, Sandy and Reds. The boys and I rode the same school bus for eight straight years. We remained in contact across the miles, even when college separated us.

It was inevitable that the call I dreaded finally came. It was Sandy on the phone, from Arizona, where he had become successful in the hotel industry.

"Dad died last night."

"I'm so sorry, Sandy."

Sandy's strong faith sustained him. "Don't be upset. It's a time of celebration. Now he'll be reunited with Mom."

"When is the service, Sandy?"

"The viewing is Friday night and the church service is Saturday morning. We're having a reception at the church social hall."

"When do you arrive?"

"Probably Wednesday. Reds and his wife are coming, too. You know, final arrangements."

"Of course. Do you folks want to stay at my house? There's plenty of room."

"Thanks, Larry, but we've already booked rooms downtown at the Lehigh Inn. But let's plan for dinner after the church service."

It was wonderful seeing both brothers again. Reds flew in from Georgia where he managed a printing company. After the church service and reception, we went out to dinner, and reminisced for hours about the good old days, swapping funny stories about life in the Lehigh Valley and about Elmo and Doris. I hated to end our informal party, but Sandy and Reds had to catch separate Sunday flights early the next day. I figured it would be months before I'd hear from them again. I was wrong.

"Someone named Sandy is calling," my secretary announced. "Says he's your friend. He sounds upset."

It was Thursday. Only five days had passed since the funeral. I reached for the phone.

"Sandy, you O.K.?"

"No," came the desperate response.

My best friend had just lost his father. What new catastrophe could have befallen him in the space of only five days?

"I need your legal help - bad," he stammered long distance from Arizona.

"Just name it, Sandy. I'll do whatever you ask."

We had lived through a lot growing up together. I couldn't ever recall such an outpouring of distress - and I had been there when he broke old lady Spencer's picture window with one fateful swing of a baseball bat.

"What's wrong?" I implored.

"See, it's like this. When Mom died last year, Dad figured he didn't need their big apartment anymore, so the retirement home agreed to move him into a furnished one bedroom assisted living unit. Reds and I put all of Mom and Dad's stuff in storage, just in case Dad ever decided to move back into a private residence or something. All their possessions have been locked up over at 'Boulevard Secured Rental' for almost a year.

"So Sunday morning before my flight, I went to the storage place and met an estimator from Amalgamated Movers. Reds and I had previously divided up what we each wanted. Most was going to him in Georgia, and some would be auctioned off. All I wanted was the dining room table and its five matching chairs. So the moving company estimator shows up and calculates the cost to ship everything to Maine where I own a log cabin.

· "So, the estimator takes measurements, and explains that there's a minimum charge. Even if I ship just five chairs and a table, they'll bill me for 2,500 pounds. Well, there's nothing I could do about that. And I had to catch a flight in an hour, so I wrote him a check on the spot. He said his driver would pick up everything the next day. Then I ran back to the church and stopped in at the rectory. Mrs. O'Flannigan answered the door. She's the old secretary with the thick glasses. A good family friend and a kind soul. Always good for a favor. So I gave her the key to the storage door, and asked her to meet the movers. I placed the table and chairs near the front for easy access. She's such a dear - she said O.K. Tuesday she met the guy as planned. Then she called me in Arizona to confirm everything went like clockwork."

"So what's the problem?" I inquired.

"Half an hour ago (sob) I got a call from my neighbor, Delroy Shimko, in Maine. He owns the log cabin next to mine. I asked him to keep an eye out for the moving van. He says 'I thought you were shipping a table and five chairs.' I said 'yes.' He says, 'Well, where do you want to put the Steinway, the washer, the dryer, refrigerator, and the bedroom suite'?"

"I didn't know what on Earth he meant. So I called kind old Mrs. O'Flannigan. She said everything went well - especially after she figured out the lock. 'Lock?' I asked.

"She says when she got to the storage place, the key jammed, so she asked the office manager to help her. He said that happened a lot, and used big bolt cutters to open the door. Then the moving guy loaded up the truck and drove off."

"Wait a minute!" I interrupted. "You're not saying - "

"Yup. I gave O'Flannigan the key to unit 198. They opened 199. She wears thick glasses, you know."

"The storage manager didn't catch the mistake?" I questioned.

"Neither did the driver. A table and chairs don't look like a grand piano to me," Sandy added. "Apparently I was dealing with Moe, Larry, and Curly."

"Whose stuff did you move?" I cross-examined.

"Who knows?" Sandy insisted, "but his Steinway is sitting outside my cabin, and they're calling for rain. Can you (sniff) help me?"

Chapter 10
Don't Forget The Piano Bench

CHAPTER 11

THE VOLUNTEER

The Northampton County Courthouse hasn't always been as sophisticated as it is today. It used to be, when you went to the bathroom, you actually had to flush the toilet all by yourself. And as you sat in the rest room, you could truly rest, because there was no speaker system paging you mid-dump.

Before they added the new government center complex, there was no cafeteria - only Joe Green - kind, soft-spoken, smile-on-his-face, unassuming Joe Green. He operated the minuscule concession stand squeezed in a corner between the recorder of deeds office and the register of wills. He had been there since before anyone could remember, patiently sitting on his stool in his make-shift wooden shanty, surrounded by his overstocked mini-airport-style gift shop. If he didn't have it, he'd get it.

"This button just fell off my..."

"Here you are, Judge. Needle and thread. Alice down at hunting licenses can sew it back on."

Joe was a tailor, a tobacconist, and a pharmacist.

"Do you have any aspirin?"

"You bet."

Joe would reach under his counter and produce the wonder drug. As money exchanged hands, Joe would turn to his faded cigar box, and find the correct change. Cash register be damned.

Candy, magazines, health aids, baked goods, soft drinks, nail polish, dental floss, glass cleaner, chewing gum, pencils - anything a courthouse employee or passing juror might need was stocked in Joe's emporium. The great and the not so great had, at one time or another, patronized his place of business, from judges to accused murderers. Each received a genuine warm smile and personalized attention.

"You have a shoe-shine kit?" the witness with scuffed footwear inquired.

"What color leather?"

"Brown."

Joe reached under his counter and produced a small brush, cloth, and polish container, all packed in a pocket-sized kit.

Joe was as familiar to courthouse employees as the front door. A "regular" would say *hello,* and Joe would immediately address the person by title or proper name, which was remarkable. Joe was blind and had been so from birth 68 years ago.

This physical challenge didn't impede him. So skilled was this merchant, if it weren't for his dark glasses and red-and-white cane, you'd never know he was blind.

Joe sold me candy bars. But he unintentionally performed a greater service. Once in a while, if my client's ship were sinking in the courtroom, I'd grumble and pout - until I passed ever-present gentle Joe in the hallway. He could hear my altered gate approaching.

"Everything O.K., Larry? You seem upset."

His genuine concern for my ridiculous problems quickly brought me back to reality.

Joe was fiercely independent and very private. Where did he live and with whom? How did he get to the courthouse day after day? How did he refurbish his supplies? One late afternoon during a heavy unrelenting rain, I inadvertently learned of the logistical complexities facing my friend.

I was waiting for a confused jury to return with its verdict. It was 4:30 and time for Joe to close up shop for the day. I ran over to grab one last candy bar, just in case the jurors deliberated through the dinner hour. Joe heard my approaching footsteps marked by a squeaky right heal.

"Your jury still out?" he inquired.

"Yes," I confirmed.

"Milky Way?"

Joe might have been blind, but he could see into my mind.

"Thanks, Joe."

"Me, too," Harold chimed in from behind. Harold was the courthouse janitor. A nice guy, but a bit of a dim bulb.

A telephone hidden under the counter rang. Joe picked up. His face turned to stone.

"That's O.K.," he responded. "I can walk home."

He reached for the two Milky Ways.

"What's the matter?" Harold asked.

"My ride can't make it. But it's not a problem. I'll walk."

"Nonsense," Harold sang out. "You'll be soaked like a rat in this rain. I'll drive you wherever you want."

Joe's face brightened. "All right. Maybe just this once."

I said good-bye to my two friends, and turned toward the courtroom.

- - - - - - - - - - - - - - - - - - -

The jury was still deliberating at 7:00 p.m., so the judge let the panel go home for the evening. We all returned the next morning at 9:00 a.m. sharp. Strange. When I passed Joe's little shop, it wasn't open, and Joe was nowhere to be found. I couldn't recall the last time he had missed a day of work. Harold limped by, his arm in a sling.

"Harold!"

"Huh? Oh, hi Larry," the preoccupied janitor faintly acknowledged.

"What happened to you!"

Harold surveyed his bandaged arm, then looked at me.

"Had an accident," he said, fumbling for the words.

"Did you fall?"

"No, not exactly. But my car is gone."

"You had an accident?"

69

"With Joe. I was taking him home. It was awful."

"Is Joe O.K.?"

"No. He sprained his back. He won't be here for a while."

"What happened?"

"I'm not sure, exactly. See, we got in my car. I drove about three blocks over to Fifth and Walnut, and stopped at the intersection like always. Then Joe said *clear on the right*, so I pulled out, and that's when the tractor trailer drove over the back of my Buick."

"Wait a minute!"

"Yeah?"

"Joe's blind!"

"Right. I wish you had been there to remind me. Anyway, while we were lying on the stretchers in the ambulance Joe explained that he hadn't heard anything coming, so he gave the all clear. I guess he isn't as good with traffic as he is with candy bars."

Chapter 11
The Volunteer

CHAPTER 12

THE DENT

It happened quite often. My father and I would go somewhere together and some well-meaning stranger would remark how much we resembled each other. Our reaction was always the same: Dad was insulted. I was disheartened. With good reason. I didn't look anything like him, thank God, and he felt the same way about me.

It's funny. Dad's been gone awhile now, but in some ways, he's still here. I've begun to sneeze and cough just like him, and my hair has receded in the same manner. It's possible I've unintentionally acquired one or two of his other attributes.

I remember when Dove, the manufacturer of soap bars, ran an inane ad campaign with mother-daughter look-a-likes to promote its product.

Off-screen announcer: Are you two sisters?

Mother: No (blush...blush) I'm her mother, but thanks for the compliment.

Daughter: (toothy smile) We just look alike, because our skin is so soft.

Off-screen announcer: (Astonished) What's your secret?

Mother: Dove. We wash with it every day.

I'm not sure I've ever understood the point of that commercial. Did daily use of the soap mistakenly cause the daughter to look like an old hag?

The practice of law has changed dramatically since my entry into the Bar. Discoveries in science and technology have impacted the courtroom and the pursuit of justice. When I first hung my shingle, there was no such thing as DNA chromosome testing and blood profiling. Instead, we used evidence derived from less sophisticated means.

- - - - - - - - - - - - - - - - - - - -

It was June of 1974. I had been representing clients for all of eight months. I could now find my way to the courthouse without assistance, and my personal law library had grown to eight books. Some day I hoped to hire a secretary. Someone was knocking at the door. I walked through both my personal office and the reception area, the two rooms that comprised my entire leased space, and opened the door.

"Are you the lawyer?"

She was young, perhaps 17. The infant nestled in her arms could not have been more than a few weeks old.

"Are you the lawyer?" she repeated. There was desperation in her voice.

I motioned for her to enter. When was her last meal?

"They sent me over here."

"Who sent you?"

"The lady at the courthouse."

"O.K. Please sit down."

"They said maybe you could help." She started to cry.

This was the first woman to have ever cried in my office. I was unprepared. They don't teach you in law school that clients in need of representation may, on occasion, involuntarily and without warning, instantly bawl. Similarly, no one had taught me that an unannounced appearance of a crying woman usually meant complex litigation for which I could expect to break my back and get paid nothing.

"Will...(sob)...you...(sob)...help...(sob)...me?"

I was still looking for a box of tissues. I made a mental note to purchase a month's supply. (I've had a running stock ever since.)

"Of course I will," I assured her, not yet knowing for what duty had I just volunteered.

"But I have no money to...(sob)...pay you."

"That's O.K.," I said as I handed her the decorative handkerchief I found in my shirt pocket. Oh well, I never really used it. It was like the doilies in my grandmother's house - just for show.

She was beginning to breathe normally again, so I asked her some questions.

"What is your name?"

"Wendy...Wendy McMurtry."

"Is that your baby?" I pointed at the infant who had been sleeping soundly through all the turmoil.

"Yes. This is Zachariah. He's three weeks old," she announced proudly.

"What can I do for you?"

"His father says he isn't the father. He refuses to pay support. I need money for diapers and formula."

She started to cry again.

Things were starting to come into focus. The father was your run-of-the-mill deadbeat dad.

"What's the father's name?"

"Billy. Actually, it's William Sommers. But everyone calls him Billy."

"Are you folks married?"

"No."

"Does the baby carry your last name or the father's?"

"Mine. Billy wasn't around when Zachariah was born."

"Where is Billy now?"

"Driving a truck, I guess. He drives cross-country." She turned her big green eyes in my direction.

A paternity trial! She wanted me to prove that Billy was the father of her son.

"Miss McMurtry, are you single?"

"Yes."

"Never married?"

"No."

"How do you know he's the father?"

"There were no others. He's the father. A woman knows these things."

I believed my newest indigent client. For a moment, I thought about my old man. He may have burdened me with his looks, but at least he stepped up to the plate raising me and my brothers. Billy would have to be brought to justice.

Wendy had no parents or relatives. I made arrangements with the local food bank and church to assist her and the infant with necessities. Then I began the search for Billy. He worked for a household moving company. He helped load home furnishings into a van, and delivered them across the country. I caught up with him after his return from Mississippi. I stopped by the warehouse loading dock to introduce myself. The foreman pointed to some kid lifting a sofa into the back of a truck.

"You Billy?" I inquired.

The kid turned toward me, sweat streaming down his face - a face with remarkable and dramatic features. There was a deep dimple-dent below his lower lip, accentuating a chin that would rival all the greats - Lawrence Olivier, Cary Grant, Tyrone Power, and Kirk Douglas. Without a chin dent, you'd fail as a matinee idol.

Billy sported thick, blond curly hair. His high cheekbones gave way to deep-set yellow eyes. Never before had I met someone with yellow eyes. He looked like a tiger about to pounce.

I advised him why I was there.

"No way, man. That kid ain't mine."

"How can you be so sure?"

"I only spent one night with her. I bet there were plenty of guys. I ain't payin'."

And so the long journey toward a paternity trial began. I drafted a complaint, had the sheriff serve it upon Billy, who hired a lawyer to deny the allegations. A trial date was ultimately set.

Four months had passed since Wendy's first appearance at my office. There was now a degree of stability in her life. She had found part-time employment and temporary day care for Zachariah. The week before the trial

75

date, she met with me after work. I reviewed all the questions I planned to ask her. Her responses were coherent and believable. She again assured me Billy was our man.

- - - - - - - - - - - - - - - - - - -

"All rise," the tipstaff announced.

Judge Williams entered the courtroom on cue and took his position at the front of the chamber, facing those assembled before him.

"You may be seated," the tipstaff announced. The 12 jurors, witnesses, and spectators followed that directive, with the exception of one notable bystander, who was asleep. Wendy had been unable to find a baby-sitter for Zachariah, who slept under a blanket in a carriage she gently rocked next to the plaintiff's table where we both sat. Once in a while he would stir.

I planned to put Wendy on the stand first, to testify under oath that she had only had relations with Billy. Other character witnesses were prepared to confirm that my client had no other boyfriends.

"Counsel, are we ready to proceed?" His Honor inquired.

I was about to answer in the affirmative, but at that moment, Zachariah woke with a start and began to scream. His mother stepped in. She reached under the blanket and uncovered the child, who was no longer a newborn. He was nearly five months old.

I had not seen Zachariah since his first visit to my office when he was just weeks old. He reminded me then of Dwight Eisenhower - round-faced and bald. He had changed considerably since then. His curly blond hair had filled in. He had high cheekbones and piercing yellow eyes. With the exception of only one other human being, I had never seen yellow eyes before. Most remarkably, he had a notable dent in the middle of his chin, just like several movie stars and just like his old man.

"Nice lookin' kid," Judge Williams wisely noted. "Why not introduce him to the jury."

I picked up ol' Zach by his armpits, and walked over to the jury panel.

"Goo," he testified.

The jurors noticed the dent, hair, eyes, and cheekbones. Then they all shifted their gaze toward the defense table.

Billy's attorney decided not to waste the court's time. Wendy didn't have to testify and she was awarded child support on the spot. After we left the courtroom, Billy met Zachariah for the first time, to see what else they might have in common.

Chapter 12
The Dent

CHAPTER 13

I'VE CHANGED MY MIND

Our local courthouse and a nuclear submarine are strikingly similar. Both are designed to serve and protect the citizens who have paid taxes to construct them. There are other similarities. Neither maintains an exterior exhaust fan in the galley area. As a result, when eggs are cooked in the courthouse basement cafeteria, the omelette aroma works its way three flights up the elevator shaft and into Courtroom #5 even before the cook yells "Pick up!" Similar, too, is the fact that every square inch of the courthouse is claimed and inhabited. Peek into any corner, and you'll have located someone's little kingdom, the turf of which is fiercely protected.

The county commissioners control the purse strings, so they grab the best quarters - the exclusive penthouse suites with plush carpets hidden away on the fourth floor. Most of the judges do O.K., too. With seniority comes privilege, and so as new "junior judges" are elected and ascend to the bench, the older judges move up the ladder to claim courtrooms that have windows. Presiding in a windowless courtroom can be claustrophobic, much like being in a submarine. Maybe it's 3:00 a.m., maybe it's 3:00 p.m. - Who can tell?

No territory, however, is more sacred or more aggressively defended than the reserved parking spaces in the underground courthouse parking deck. Most of us undeserving wretches have never experienced the joy of displaying a vehicular reservation pass on our bumpers. It's a mystery how the "touchables" were chosen, or who decided the order in which their job titles appear on the concrete walls, next to the signs that proclaim "Reserved Parking - Tow Away Zone."

It is possible to find some degree of due process in the courtroom. An accused murderer will be permitted on occasion to tell his side of the story. Not so in the parking deck. A few foolhardy souls have actually dared to trespass upon spaces marked as sacred. With one or two exceptions, neither they nor their vehicles have ever been seen again.

Closest to the underground courthouse secret entrance are six spaces for the county commissioners. These guys show up about once a month for important county council meetings. The rest of the time, those spaces sit vacant. Next are the judges. The senior judge parks closest to the county commissioners. The other judges' spots are based upon the date each jurist was elected to the bench. If two were elected on the same day, preference goes to the candidate who received more votes.

Next come the county detectives. They may search for crimes, but never for spaces. The pecking order continues with the district attorney, fiscal operations director, prothonotary, sheriff, recorder of deeds, clerk of criminal courts, warden, public defender, bridge inspector, director of computer control, probation, veterans affairs, jury panel, voting registrar, office of weights and measures, health inspector, register of wills, and 72 reserved spaces later, at the end of the parking deck, concludes with the county forester. The rest of us who have no dignitary bumper stickers must fend for ourselves. Hundreds of jurors, having been called to duty, circle the courthouse similar to a wagon train. When these conscripted citizens finally stumble through the courthouse door, breathless, the director of the jury panel (parking space #56) admonishes them for daring to arrive late.

The district attorney and his twelve assistant district attorneys maintain offices in the southwest corner of the second floor of the courthouse addition. This section was added to the original courthouse about 10 years ago at a cost of $36 million to the taxpayers. The move was an attempt to assure there would be sufficient space for everyone.

Trouble is, they built the addition where the public parking lot used to be. A short five years later, it dawned on the county planning officials that the courthouse was once again short on parking. So, in a flash of brilliance, they moved the domestic relations office with its staff of 80, and the office of children and youth, with its staff of 50, five blocks away into the newly created downtown courthouse annex - a massive red brick structure that had, a century before, been a thriving blouse mill. It was thought the relocation would help both to create more space at the courthouse, and to revitalize the depressed downtown area. Surprisingly, the transition of 130 office workers and the countless clientele they serviced, only proved to further aggravate the already congested downtown parking situation.

The office of the public defender is located in the courthouse one floor above the district attorney's office. Fifteen defense counsel represent indigents accused of various crimes. Unfortunately, the architect who failed to provide an exhaust fan for the cafeteria also failed to design a location where the multitude of private attorneys retained by paying clients might meet before trial to prepare their cases. Not a single conference room exists for the convenience of the public. As a result, scores of attorneys and clients awaiting their hour in court are forced to meet and discuss strategy in the cafeteria.

Ironically, there is a benefit to this architectural oversight. During criminal court week, members of the county's defense bar are able to mingle together in the cafeteria and learn from shared stories and experiences. As an example, last month's criminal court week started out like any other. It was a Tuesday, the second day of the trial list and barely 8:00 in the morning. I parked just 11 blocks from the courthouse after finding a convenient spot where cars are rarely vandalized. The courthouse had not yet come to life. I walked into the cafeteria hoping to find my client. Instead I found Bernie O'Shaughnessy, the undisputed patriarch of the defense bar. Similar to some fabled gunslinger of old, Bernie had, over the past 40 years, successfully fought off countless indictments, informations, and grand jury charges filed against hundreds of his clients. He had gained so many acquittals that criminal defendants flocked to his office from miles around.

Bernie represented, for those he defended, the only ray of hope standing between them, the Constitution, and jail. The Commonwealth of Pennsylvania could call upon an array of law enforcement officers, detectives, and prosecutors. Bernie, armed with piercing blue eyes and a baritone voice that emanated from somewhere within a 5-foot 7-inch 140-pound frame, faced this army without fear.

So, true to his character, Bernie parked wherever the hell he wanted. And no one ever said a word - not a judge, not the courthouse security rent-a-cops, nor the tow truck guy.

I often wondered if his intimidating voice was God given, or whether it was derived from 40 years of chain smoking. Try though he may, he couldn't quit. And in his later years, stopped caring. There he sat in the cafeteria, positioned directly below the "No Smoking" sign, a non-filtered camel dangling from his lips.

"It won't be this cigarette that kills me, counsellor," he said, reading my mind. He motioned for me to sit and join him. The month before, he had had a cancerous tumor the size of a baseball removed from his neck. He was out of the hospital on the third day conducting business from his bed at home.

As we sat together, Bernie turned his attention to a Bar Association Journal article he had been studying.

"Will you look at this load of manure," he moaned. "Some quack is now recommending psychological profiling of jurors. And this is supposed to help us pick the right people to serve on a jury?" He began to laugh.

"Doesn't screening have its benefits?" I offered.

"Listen, Larry. Who knows what the hell a juror thinks until the evidence is presented? It's a crap shoot. A juror can focus in on something you'd never imagine. From a defense perspective, that's the beauty of the jury system - one stubborn off-the-wall juror can spin the whole process."

A few other lawyers were starting to make their way into the cafeteria, including Dottie Gridlow and Chris Spengler, a couple of assistant district attorneys looking for coffee. They plopped down uninvited at our table. Dottie could be pleasant or a complete bitch. It all depended on the lunar cycle. She began the sales pitch of the day.

"Larry..."

"Yes?"

"You represent Billy Tuchi?"

"You know I do," I said

"Whatever. Do your client a favor and take a plea to theft. He might get probation. If this case goes to trial, I'll include the burglary and conspiracy charges, and the son-of-a-bitch will end up in jail for stealing a lousy TV set."

Her offer was enticing, but unpersuasive.

"My guy says he's innocent. Why don't you just drop the charges and save everyone the hassle?"

Dottie mustered up her best assistant district attorney smirk, and turned to Chris.

"Chris, I have a hairdresser appointment this afternoon. Of course, this case is a slam-dunk and Fox and his soon to be incarcerated client both know it. Do me a favor, Love, and take the file. I think the judge will want to start picking a jury right after lunch."

Chris balked at the prospect of inheriting a case at the last minute - a case in which he had neither interviewed the witnesses, nor studied the prior preliminary hearing transcript. Dottie put him at ease.

"Not to worry. It's a 10-minute trial with only one witness. See, Tuchi entered Goodwin's Cash and Carry Store over on Fourth Street, and carried out a TV set without presenting the cash. The security guard caught him red-handed."

Dottie again turned in my direction for dramatic effect. "A slam dunk," she repeated. "Chris, if you do this little 10-minute favor for me, I'll take your next trial off your hands. I'm just desperate for a cut and color."

"A slam dunk," Chris pondered aloud. "Even if my next trial takes a week and there are dozens of witnesses?"

"Yup, I'll take it," Dottie confirmed with a nod.

Chris turned to me. "Looks like you and I will be doing business this afternoon," he advised. Soon he was on his way to the DA's office. He'd need to study the file, and interview his witness.

Sure enough, the judge announced that our 10-minute trial would commence right after lunch. So I located my client, who had just finished visiting some of his friends at the county prison, and completed last minute preparations for his pending court appearance. I advised Tuchi of his latest options.

"The DA says if you plead guilty to theft, you'll likely get probation. Otherwise, if you go to trial, and are convicted of all the charges, you may end up in jail."

"You ever done time, Fox?" Tuchi inquired.

"Jail time?"

"Yup."

"No."

"It ain't that bad. You get to be with your pals, away from the old lady, and they feed you grub three times a day. Once in a while you play a game of hoops, then you take a nap. Next morning, they bring breakfast right to your cell."

I couldn't recall service that good at Club Med.

"So if I lose, I don't. Get it? Trial don't scare me. Jail don't scare me," Tuchi said with a yawn. Apparently, neither did the security guards at Goodwin's Cash & Carry.

Trial started promptly at 1:30 with the picking of a jury. A psychological evaluation of the jury panel would have been helpful, so I might have known which jurors to reel in, and which to throw back. But the black and white TV set Tuchi had allegedly stolen cost just $48 retail, so he probably wasn't prepared to cough up $20,000 for a comprehensive study. I decided to do my own on-the-spot analysis.

Let's see...The lady with the two chins, blue hair and fake pearls looked sorta like my grandmother's next-door neighbor who was always sweet and forgiving. She's on.

The guy with the cheap rug and beady eyes is giving me bad vibes. He's off.

The kid with the long hair, diamond stud in his nose and fake tan seems like he would be capable of lifting a TV. He's on. Psychologist? Who needs a psychologist?

The district attorney put on his one and only witness, Stanley, the part-time security guard.

"Tell the jury what happened," Chris inquired.

Stanley cleared his throat, causing his enlarged Adam's apple to bob up and down three times along the entire length of his giraffe-like neck. I hadn't seen anything like that since Stiles Levan had taken a dare back in eighth grade from Ida Wida to eat a golf ball.

The lady with the blue hair stopped fidgeting with her pearls, and began to concentrate on the traveling Adam's apple. Similar to the spectators at a tennis game, everyone's eyes now followed in synchronization as this portion of Stanley's anatomy involuntarily ascended and descended. I doubted if anyone was listening to Stanley.

"Well ya see, (bob up) this guy entered (bob down) Goodwin's Cash (bob up) & Carry, picked up a TV, (bob down) and walked out (bob up) the store without paying."

"Is the perpetrator in the courtroom?" Chris inquired.

"Yes. The per (bob up) pet (bob down) trat (bob up) or is seated at the defense table." Stanley's outstretched finger and his Adam's apple both pointed at Tuchi. Did the jury even notice whom the witness had identified?

I had very little to ask Stanley, so the jury received its instructions, and retired to deliberate. I figured a verdict would be returned against Tuchi in about 15 minutes, and 14 minutes of that would consist of an argument among the jurors as to who should be foreperson.

Five hours rolled by. I could hear Chris wriggling in his seat at the prosecutor's table. He kept muttering something to himself about slam-dunks and hair salons. Tuchi had fallen asleep on one of the courtroom benches, dreaming of future basketball games with his incarcerated friends, followed by room service. A slight smile graced his angelic face.

"The jury has reached a verdict," the bailiff announced.

Tuchi instinctively sat up and rubbed his eyes. Chris began to twitch faster. The jury marched back in, and the judge reappeared on cue.

"Have you reached a unanimous verdict?" his honor inquired.

Some guy I couldn't recall putting on the jury stood up. "We have, Your Honor."

"As to the count of retail theft, what say you?"

The foreman was about to respond. After all, he knew what to do from his vast experience watching TV. But before he could open his mouth, the lady with the blue hair rose from her seat as she desperately clutched her pearls. It was one of those surrealistic moments when the universe stops spinning, the clocks stop ticking, and Justice peeks through the windows.

"I've changed my mind," she confessed. "I don't think he's guilty any more. The district attorney didn't introduce evidence of fingerprints. Don't you gotta have fingerprints?"

That logic was sufficient enough for the kid with the diamond stud in his nose. He stood up, too.

"Yeah, there weren't no fingerprints put in evidence. I've changed my mind, too."

Tuchi appeared slightly disappointed. While in theory he might be able to keep the TV set, he had yet to write in for the 1-year limited warranty. Chris seemed upset as well, as he searched in his thin slam-dunk file for fingerprint photos. The judge looked confused as he abruptly left the bench.

Ms. Blue Hair was still standing in the jury box. "Did I say something wrong?" she called out after the judge.

"Not at all," I assured her. "Not at all."

One week later, I happened to pass Dottie in the hall. She had a lovely new 'do, but it was barely visible, since she was carrying a ton of ADA files.

Chapter 13

I've Changed My Mind

CHAPTER 14

THE BOX

I doubt I will ever forget Erma Zipf.

"That's *Zipf*," she corrected me.

"Zipf," I repeated perfectly, following her inflection and mimicking her intonation.

"*Zipf*," she repeated. "The emphasis is on the 'p,' not the 'f.' Now try it again."

"Z i P f."

"No, Zipf," she observed once again.

Her fourth floor apartment was small and sweltering. It didn't help that I had chosen to walk up the fire exit stairs. It was either that, or the elevator, which was devoid of a current inspection certificate. By the time she answered her door, I was dripping with sweat.

"Air costs money," she explained.

I took a silent oath I'd never again make another house call even if the client were on a ventilator.

"I understand you want to write your last will and testament, Mrs. Zipf."

"That's *Zipf*. The emphasis is on the - "

"That's right," a Ms. Downsucker confirmed as she sat in the cramped apartment. "She needs a last will and testament."

Downsucker. Come to think of it, I wasn't too pleased with her. She was the one who got me into this hot hellhole mess.

"My next door neighbor is very ill and needs you to put her affairs in order," she had explained over the phone. "Can you come right away?"

So I went. And there I sat, the clock ticking and messages accumulating back at the office. I turned away from Downsucker.

"I understand you want to write your last will and testament, *Erma*."

"Is that what I want? Is that why you're here? What's your name?"

"Mrs. Zipf, your neighbor here, Ms. Downsucker, called me saying that you wanted to draft a will."

"I do? Do I need a will?" Zipf asked me.

"Of course you do, Erma," a concerned Downsucker interrupted. "Remember how we talked about you being so up in age. And how you might die some day. And how you don't have any family. And how you got to write down who gets your stuff when you die? Remember?"

"Did we talk about that?"

"Sure we did. And that's when you said I could have some of your things here in the apartment that I particularly like, being as how we have been neighbors for over a year and all, and that I'm such a good friend. Remember?"

"Ms. Downsucker..."

"Yes?"

"When I conduct an interview, I prefer to meet with my client...alone. You know...privately?"

"Oh! You want me to leave. Right. I understand. I'll just be going now so you two can get acquainted."

She slowly rose from the Spartan combination living room - dining room - kitchen, and grabbed for her oversized handbag. "I'm leaving, Erma."

"Where you going?"

"Next door. The nice lawyer here is gonna talk to you."

"He is?"

"Now *remember* what we discussed. O.K.?"

"O.K.," Zipf said blankly.

We sat alone, my new client and I, in the dismal apartment with no air conditioning. Zipf was wearing a wool cardigan.

"Mind if I take off my suit coat?" I inquired.

"Go right ahead."

So many old and forgotten people. So much elder abuse. So common.

"Mrs. Zipf..."

"*Zipf.* It's *Zipf...*"

"Does anyone help you with your food or cleaning?"

"The Meals on Wheels. They come just about every day."

"Do you have any family to look in on you?"

"Family?"

"Any children?"

"No. No children. My husband died in the Korean War just after we got married."

"What did you do for a living?"

"Blouse mill. I was a sewing machine operator for 38 years. I'm retired 20 years now."

I decided to rescind my selfish oath. I was glad Downsucker had called. She had unwittingly done Zipf a favor. I now intended to make sure that Zipf's few paltry assets go where she intended - beyond the scheming grasp of her neighbor.

"Mrs. Zipf..."

I waited to be corrected...

"It's *Zipf...*"

"Do you have a last will?"

"I don't think so. What is that?"

I decided to travel a different road.

"Do you have any family or friends?"

She became thoughtful. "I did, you know. Once. There were about six of us who would play cards. Do you play? Anyway, they're all dead, or in nursing homes, I think. No one comes to visit me anymore."

"Ms. Downsucker mentioned that you had certain possessions. What is she talking about?"

"It's mine."

"What's yours?"

"My box."

"Your safe-deposit box?"

"No. The box. It's under my bed."

"Does Downsucker know about the box?"

"I think so. She talks about it when she's here."

"May I see it?"

90

"You can't have it either. It's mine."

"I agree. If I promise not to take anything, may I look in the box?"

"Maybe, as long as you don't take stuff."

Zipf struggled as she tried to extricate herself from a tattered olive-green upholstered chair. I followed as she inched her way into the bedroom.

"It's down there," she pointed.

I lifted the corner of a torn blanket, and peered under the bed. There, I found a large cardboard box, covered with almost one-quarter inch of dust. I dragged the box into the murky daylight, and placed it on the bed. It must have weighed 15 pounds. I folded back the cardboard cover, and exposed the lid to an ornate jewelry box.

"Let me get that," Zipf ordered.

I stood aside. My hostess gently raised the container from its protective packaging, and placed the silver receptacle onto the bed. She opened the lid.

What sat before me looked like a private collection of the crown jewels. There were several diamond rings, necklaces, and earrings. The stones on each were huge and looked to be of high quality. Several pendants, broaches, and stickpins were decorated with opals, rubies, and other precious gems. There were two other legal-size envelopes in the bottom of the carton.

"For a rainy day," she explained. "In case I want to go shopping or something."

One envelope contained more than 200 early American proof set gold coins. The other housed more than $100,000 in $100 bills. The bills were at least 50 years old.

"Where did all this - "

"From my parents. They told me not to squander it. I haven't."

I returned everything to the cardboard box, just as it had been stored. Mrs. Zipf watched with an attentive eye, as I placed the box gently under her bed. We returned to the living room. The air was thick and my stomach was tied in knots.

"Mrs. Zipf..."

"Zipf..."

"Zipf...the contents of this box should be sealed in a bank vault. It is unwise to keep such valuables here."

"Banks fail. My things stay with me in case I need them. I don't get around so easy nowadays."

Further attempts to educate Zipf failed. I decided to leave.

"Come back next week, will you?" she suggested. "People. It's nice seeing people. We can talk then."

So, I promised to return. Back at the office, I researched the law regarding involuntary guardianship, then I called the county president judge, and explained the situation.

"That's a tough one, Larry," Judge Williams confirmed. "You have a couple of problems. First, a doctor must testify that she is incapacitated and in need of third party intervention. I'm not sure she has fallen into that category yet. Moreover, you obtained these insights in your capacity as her private counsel. That's privileged information. Furthermore, even if you could testify, there's caselaw that suggests you may have a direct conflict of interest if you assist in imposing an involuntary guardianship on your own client. Simply put, people in this country have the right to store their assets in their homes, even though a bank might provide better safeguards."

His Honor was correct, but something about this case gave me the creeps. Downsucker was a threat to my client. But I could only contact Zipf by calling Downsucker, because Zipf had no telephone. "They cost too much and I got nobody to talk to," she had advised me.

I had promised Zipf I would return in a week. I tried repeatedly to call Downsucker. There was no answer. I stopped by the apartment complex and knocked on Zipf's door.

"Who are you?" Charlie, a maintenance man, inquired.

"Mrs. Zipf's lawyer."

"She ain't here."

"When do you expect her back?"

"Don't know. She had a stroke or something. She's in the hospital. Meals on Wheels found her. She was on the floor mumbling something about a box."

Why hadn't Downsucker notified me? I banged on her door.

"She ain't there neither," Charlie offered.

"When is she coming back?"

"She's not. She cleaned out her apartment about the time Zipf took sick. Didn't even give a forwarding address to send her mail. Her lease ain't up yet."

I convinced my guide to open Zipf's apartment. Everything appeared untouched. I looked under the bed. The box was gone. That afternoon I contacted the police. They filed the obligatory report.

Zipf died a week later, her jewelry unrecovered.

Chapter 14
The Box

CHAPTER 15

THE ADOPTION

It had been a stressful day. Any day spent in family support court is aggravating, counter-productive and dehumanizing. This morning I had represented Merlin Goober who finally conceded, after the paternity tests were completed, that three of his girlfriend's children were probably his. Chelsea had other children before and after Merlin. But he was the true love of her life - until he declined to pay child support.

As I stood before the judge with Merlin by my side, I wondered if his honor was as disillusioned with the system as was I. Seventeen similar cases of derelict parents had been reviewed by the court prior to Merlin's 15-minute appearance, and as I looked back at the spectator pews, it appeared that 70 or 80 more bums would find their way up to the bench before day's end. Judge Yancy had been presiding over "Happy Court" for almost three years. He had been forced to listen as thousands of dead-beat parents concocted stories to suggest why they shouldn't have the responsibility to feed or cloth their children. How had the judge remained sane?

It was Merlin's opportunity to explain why he didn't have to care for his offspring.

"See, Judge, it's like this. I lost my job over at the gas station, and then she kicked me out of the - "

"When?"

"When what?"

"When did you lose your job?"

"About a year ago."

"What have you been doing since then?"

"Lookin' for another one."

"How have you survived without a job?"

"Well, my new girlfriend, she works as an assistant manager over at the - "

"Mr. Goober..."

"Yes?"

"You've got one week to find gainful full-time employment. If you fail in that search, and your child support payments are still in arrears, you will be incarcerated, after which employment will be found for you under the supervision of the prison work release program."

"But Judge, you don't understand, it ain't easy trying to find a job that - "

"Listen, mister, I'm also imputing an earning capacity based upon your excellent state of health and job-related skills whereby you shall pay $40 per week for each child, retroactive to the date when the support petition was filed. By my calculation, you now owe the domestic relations office $1,480, and each week that sum will grow by $120."

Merlin turned to me in desperation.

"Can't you do something?" he pleaded.

Merlin was this month's pro bono client assigned by the Bar Association. I was glad I hadn't taken a legal fee. I wondered whether his children would eat an adequate meal that night.

It was good to return to the solitude of my office, far away from the Merlins of the world. For a moment or two, I gazed out the window. Why had God blessed me with parents who had spent their last dimes to ensure I obtained the best education possible? Why had I grown up in a home where there was always food and loving attention at the ready? The office intercom was buzzing.

"There's a Mrs. Perryman calling," my secretary announced.

"Has she been here before?"

"The name doesn't sound familiar."

I picked up the phone. "This is Larry Fox. May I help you?"

"This is Mrs. Perryman...June Perryman."

There was a nervous upbeat excitement in her voice. Maybe a new home purchase. It was rare anyone ever called with good news.

"It's nice to make your acquaintance," I said.

"I'll get right to the point, Mr. Fox. One of my friends at church said you assist with adoptions. Is that true?"

Five times before in my career I had received a similar animated inquiry. Five times before I had sworn I'd never again make the same mistake. Handling an adoption is similar to feeding a pet rattlesnake. Things can quickly go wrong without warning. A chill ran down my spine.

"Are you still there?"

"Yes...Yes, I am."

"You worked on the adoption for Mr. and Mrs. Beanstoffer, right? They go to our church."

I doubt I'd ever forget that fiasco. When the baby was born, its skin color suggested the real father wasn't the guy whose name was on the birth certificate. Then I had to fight with a hospital social worker, who was trying to persuade the 16-year-old mother to change her mind and keep the baby.

"Mrs. Perryman, I don't really..."

"This will be the most important thing my husband and I ever do. And the Beanstoffers said you're patient, kind, and sympathetic."

"Mrs. Perryman..."

"With your help, our three lives will be forever affected for the better. We need your help."

I could hear her choking back tears. Rats! That's the problem with adoptions. One minute the client is ecstatic, the next she's devastated. And just like the natural mother, the adopting mother will ultimately experience her own form of labor pains. It happens every time. And then there are the 4:00 a.m. phone calls to see if the baby has arrived. Every baby to have ever been adopted shows up at 4:00 a.m.

"If you do this for us, you'll be forever in our prayers and the prayers of our future child," she confided.

Neither Merlin Goober, nor the thousands of other worthless goobers dodging the responsibilities of parenthood had ever tendered such a heartfelt promise in my direction.

"Mrs. Perryman..."

"Yes (sob)..."

"I would be pleased to assist you."

My newest client regained her composure and explained how motherhood now loomed large on the horizon.

"See, we've been trying for almost 10 years. Then, last week, Dr. Blackman told me about one his patients, Lucinda. She's a freshman in college, unmarried, and pregnant. She wants her baby to have a good home. The doctor said we should contact a lawyer right away."

Good advice. The transition of an innocent new life from natural parents to the comforting arms of adopting parents required intervention and monitoring by the court. Nothing could be left to chance.

I located the natural father, Jeffrey, or more precisely, the natural father-to-be, a kid in the same graduating class as Lucinda. Both natural parents agreed to subject themselves to the requisite battery of psychological testing and court-mandated interviews to confirm that they understood the significance of the proposed adoption. My clients, the Perrymans, underwent similar evaluation. County detectives questioned their friends, employers, and relatives. Financial and criminal background checks were performed. Military service, religious upbringing, educational background - an entire life's history was presented to the court for review.

The selling of a baby is a criminal offense. Assisting a pregnant mother is, on the other hand, quite legal. Lucinda needed maternity clothes and other essentials. The Perrymans paid for everything. Luckily, Lucinda possessed insurance coverage through her parents' plan, since she was still an unemancipated student maintaining the same address as her parents. As a result, the cost of almost all pre-natal care was covered. The pregnancy appeared to be normal, and free of complications.

As is often the case with a first-time pregnancy, Lucinda's labor did not begin until three days after her due date. With the onset of contractions, she was admitted to St. Joseph's Hospital. My clients were kept advised of every stage of the hospitalization. They could not contain their joy. Tests had recently determined that the fetus was male, so the Perrymans purchased a couple of gallons of robin's egg blue paint, and put the finishing touches on the baby's room.

It was about 4:00 in the morning when I got the call from the hospital. The baby was on its way.

"I'll be right there," I assured the social worker, who needed my presence as court-appointed intermediary. Good to my word, I telephoned the Perrymans, and advised them of the blessed event. Their early morning excitement was contagious.

"We're on our way," Mrs. Perryman sang out.

The hospital security guard gave me a special ID pass for the fourth floor maternity ward. Entering this restricted area brought back recollections of adoptions that had long since silently passed into history - of little lives that had experienced radical changes in direction during their brief journey from one side of the maternity ward to the other. It was all coming back to me, those suppressed memories of subdued lighting, infants in incubators, and blinking monitors. Some of the squirming humans I had carried out of here probably had kids of their own by now. And carry them I had. It was strict hospital policy that I, as court-appointed intermediary, physically take the baby from its mother, and deliver it to the waiting adopting parents. On occasion I had driven the new arrival to its new home. On other occasions, my security-pass-less clients had met me on the other side of the maternity ward door.

"Are you Mr. Fox?" the tired nurse inquired. She had a right to be tired. It was 4:30 in the morning.

"Yes," I confirmed as she squinted at my temporary ID tag.

"Dr. Philips would like to see you over at the nurses' station."

I followed her past two other unsmiling nurses. The low-intensity lighting surrounded their faces with a somber, blue tint. I felt as if I were in church, so I, like everyone else, began to whisper.

I didn't hear any babies crying. Weren't there supposed to be babies crying?

"This is Dr. Philips," the nurse motioned as she walked away. Philips didn't look up. He was busy writing official records. I was back at Coast Guard boot camp. Senior personnel would always make you stand around for a minute or two without eye contact for greater dramatic affect.

"Hello?" I softly announced. I had not whispered out of respect for Philips who still labored at his record keeping. I whispered because I sensed that God had just entered the nurses' station, and I wanted to display proper manners toward Him. After all, a new life was about to experience a radical transformation.

"Mr. Fox?"

"Yes."

"Dick Philips." He stuck out his hand. "Pull up a chair."

I shook his hand and reached for a seat.

"Baby Boy X was born at 4:05 this morning. Seven pounds, two ounces," he advised.

What a way to be born - known only as "X" - waiting for strangers you've never even met to give you a name.

"I'm pleased to hear that," I whispered. God was pleased to hear the news as well, I'm sure.

"I've just completed some preliminary tests. There's nothing conclusive yet, but it is possible Baby Boy X has, in layman's terms, a defective heart valve. We won't know for sure until he's transported down to Children's Hospital in Philadelphia for more tests, but the chances are good he will need immediate surgery."

The significance of this disclosure was just beginning to penetrate my early morning brain. "Open heart surgery," I gasped.

"There's an in-coming helicopter ready to transport the baby. How do you wish to proceed?"

"How do *I* wish..." I stammered.

"Are you the court-appointed intermediary?"

"Yes."

"O.K. It's your kid. Do you want him air-lifted? Philadelphia is standing by with a prepped O.R."

"Wait a minute...Wait a minute, Doctor. Why am I making medical decisions about the care of this baby? You're the doctor."

"But I'm not the insurance company," Philips responded.

"I beg your pardon? It's 4:30 in the morning, and my mind isn't entirely in gear just yet. Doesn't the natural mother, Lucinda, have insurance coverage through her parents? All the court papers confirm there's full coverage."

"Correct. For Lucinda. But she signed the preliminary papers giving up the baby. Baby X doesn't belong to her any more. He belongs to..."

"Wait a minute!" I blurted out. "You mean to tell me that - "

"All of Lucinda's costs are covered. Baby X, however, is a different issue."

I sat in stunned silence. "So if I don't give the O.K., the child may die?"

"Not exactly. If you don't want the baby, the County Office of Children and Youth will be contacted, and they may give approval. But if they give consent, the taxpayers of this county will probably want to keep the baby."

Philips was, of course, correct. If the county had to pay to save the child's life, the county would take custody and ultimately determine any future placement of the infant.

I looked up to ask God for advice, but instead fixed upon the faces of Mr. and Mrs. Perryman, their noses pressed up upon the outer windows of the locked doors leading into the maternity ward. They stood separated from their new baby by less than a few hundred feet. I turned back to Philips.

"Doctor, what are the chances of successful heart surgery?"

"Won't know 'til they're in there."

"What's the cost?"

"The helicopter ride will cost more than a new car. If you gotta ask, you can't afford it."

"Doctor..."

"Yes..."

˙ "How much time do I have to make a decision?"

"The baby's condition is critical. Every minute's delay is critical."

The Perrymans caught sight of me and began to wave exuberantly. Mrs. Perryman was surrounded by blue balloons. She was both laughing and crying, emotions I might soon display as well.

"I have to discuss this with my clients."

"I understand," the physician offered.

"Will you join us, in case they have any medical questions?"

"Certainly."

I slowly stood up, and turned to walk down the hallway. The Perrymans were still waving frantically. Would they want a baby born with a heart condition? Would they pay a fortune to authorize the open-heart surgery? They were people of modest means. How far could love for an infant they had not yet seen be stretched? I waited for the hand of God to push me toward my ecstatic clients.

Chapter 15
The Adoption

CHAPTER 16

WRONG CENTURY

There are those unfortunate individuals for whom nothing is funny. Ever. They have no favorite joke. They can't tell a humorous story. Their faces are permanently set in a frown.

Mr. Candell was inching his aged body up the law office steps. I had offered a home consultation, but he declined.

"You charge for travel time? I'm 97! Forget it!" I opened the oversized door for my client.

"Well, don't just stand there," he snapped. "Where can I sit down?"

I pointed down the hallway. Candell shuffled on ahead of me. Then he slid into a chair.

"Hardwood? For what I'm paying, you can't buy a seat cushion?"

"I'm sorry. Perhaps I could find you a - "

"Save it. I'm paying by the minute, so kill the chatter."

I sat down in another hard seat, admonished. Had this cantankerous old skinflint ever smiled? Had he ever intentionally gone out of his way to make someone else giggle? A life of lemons.

"My wife, Elsie, passed away 15 years ago."

"I'm sorry for your - "

"Save it. She's dead. At the time, I was still young, only 82. But my quack doctor said I had inoperable cancer, and progressive heart disease. He guaranteed I wouldn't last another six months. Fool that I was, I believed him. So I made arrangements to buy a headstone for my wife's cemetery plot and for mine. After all, the stonecutter was having a two-for-one on headstones. It meant a $35 savings if I did it all in one shot. I hate paying extra."

"Yes," I gathered.

"So the stonecutter, he asks for the wife's date of birth and date of death, and did I want it to say *Rest In Peace*. That was extra, so I passed...These seats are terrible."

"I'm sorry that - "

"Can it! How long have I been here?"

"Five minutes."

"Good. So where was I...oh yeah...so the stonecutter asks for my date of birth, and I give him that, too. Then I had a thought. Since it was already 1990, and since I was going to die anyway in a few months, could I save some more money if he carved in the numbers 199_ and left the last year of my death blank. He said O.K., and gave me a $20 discount. Well, that was a mistake."

"What do you mean?"

"What do I mean? Do I look dead to you? What year is it? Right up to midnight of December 31, 1999, when the ball slid down the tower at Times Square, I was hoping I'd drop dead. But instead, the new century arrived, my cancer went into remission, and I got a pacemaker. I lost my $20 discount on the stone."

"Mr. Candell, I'm confused. *You* didn't lose any money. The stonecutter did."

"That's what you think. So I go back to the stonecutter, and tell him to change the numbers from '199_' to '200_.' He says he can't; that the monument is made of pink quarry marble, and there's no way to patch it. He's got to cut an entirely new slab. Well I ain't paying twice to die once, so I thought about suing the doctor who gave me the bad advice."

"You can't be serious."

"Turns out he dropped dead over 10 years ago. Jogging, of all things. So I want you to sue the stonecutter."

"On what basis?"

"He carved the wrong date."

I had always thought that my neighbor, Frank, was the cheapest person on the face of the earth. Frank kept an old set of tires in his garage. They had a 1/4 inch tread left. When it came time to have his car inspected, he'd remove the bald tires, and replace them with the "good" tires he stored in the garage. After the car passed inspection, the good tires went back into storage for another year.

But Mr. Candell appeared to have taken the science of tightwaddism to a new plateau.

"But why sue the stonecutter?" I asked.

"He should've told me the marble couldn't be recarved. How was I supposed to know the doctor jumped the gun on my diagnosis?"

"Mr. Candell..."

"What?"

"I don't want your case."

"You don't?"

"No."

"Well," he said turning to leave, "don't bother sending me a bill."

Chapter 16
Wrong Century

CHAPTER 17

THE BODY BAG

My law office wasn't always a law office. Once upon a time the building served as a funeral home. Whoever designed the place was eccentric. There are 32 rooms, and each has a unique shape with different dimensions. One of my partners labors in what might have been the formal parlor for viewings. His windows are composed of stained glass and his polished wooden floor shows the wear of countless shoes shuffling in line at countless wakes. Another partner works in the adjoining spectator's area, on the other side of huge sliding pocket doors, that upon retraction, create one common area.

My office rug covers the remnants of an old tile floor. The wall has been carefully patched where plumbing fixtures once protruded. My office was the embalming room. The frosted windows were designed to keep curious eyes from looking in. Unlike the hallways serving the other first floor rooms, the passageway leading to my back office is narrow, and it is encumbered with a sharp bend to the right, where a private door opens to our back yard parking area.

After midnight, the resident ghosts begin their work in earnest. They never attempt to scare or even talk to me. They just want exercise. I generally try to leave the office before the bewitching hour, but it's not always possible. One time as I walked down the narrow hallway, my car keys in hand, one of the old-timers, a ghost named Harold (he lives in the upstairs window seat) walked past me. The hallway is only three feet wide, so we both had to turn sideways, our backs pressed against the wall. Our noses came within inches of one another as we passed in silence.

- - - - - - - - - - - - - - - - - - -

It was a typical Monday. The phones were ringing off their hooks as I conducted the usual early morning damage control of the office. Apparently, I was the first to detect a toilet running upstairs. Then I noticed that the war of the office temperatures was still being waged from the day before. The eastern half of the building was as cold as Glacier National Park, whereas the western half remained as hot as the equator. Myrtle, one of our heavier secretaries, cranks the AC to 68 degrees. Sally, our rather thin receptionist, sweater in tow, keeps her half at a balmy 84. The zones meet in my room, where life is similar to standing on the moon. Turn to your left and you'll melt. Turn to the right, and you may suffer from hypothermia.

My secretary stuck her overworked head through the door and motioned to three blinking phone lines on hold for me.

"I'm still on line two with the bank about the down payment check that didn't clear," she explained. "Line three is some guy from Illinois calling about the Edison Estate date of death values."

"Who's on four?"

"Hormly, or maybe it's Hornley. I can't tell - he's on his cell. He wants to schedule a settlement for the purchase of his new house."

And so it went. By 10:30 my stomach churned out those strange *you didn't feed me breakfast - now I'm agitated* noises. By 11:30 I swore I'd never again forget my brown-bag lunch. On the other hand, there wasn't even time to sit and actually eat, so there was only one thing left to do. My 11:55 announcement: "I'm going to the mini-mart: Anybody want anything?"

As I inched toward the door, I caught a glimpse of Cathy. She looked forlorn, the phone still stuck to her head.

"I'm on hold with a realtor," she pressed. "Did you talk to that guy Hormly about a settlement date?"

"No, he hung up while on hold. If it's important, he'll call back. Hell, he's not even the client. We represent the buyers - not the sellers. I'll call them as soon as I get back."

Great. Another power lunch - of garbage. I stepped out the narrow back hallway, raced across the parking lot and into the old gas station recently renovated (again) into a mini-mart-drug-store-bakery-dry cleaner. There had to be *something* in plain view that I could grab and eat in three minutes flat. I started toward the low-carb energy bars. And that's when I saw them: Two plump, slow-turning, aromatic hot dogs with tempting bubbly cheese to boot. Health be damned. I had to have them. I reasoned away the grease (I'd swim extra laps tonight). I reasoned away the artery-clogging cheese (calcium is good for bones). I even reasoned away the pork (who gets trichinosis these days anyway?)

I had trouble, however, reasoning away the color (mauve) and the nagging feeling that this wasn't day number one on the rotisserie spinner for these bad boys.

I scooped up the revolving delicacies with the plastic wiener tongs chained to the grill. (I've found that important things like wiener tongs and pens at bank teller windows are always chained.) I placed the two glistening dogs in two high-carb, super-refined, mini-mart buns. The guy standing in the glass booth next to the cash register smirked.

"You like dem...how you say...cheese dogs, eh?"

"How much?" I replied.

"Foo-o-twee, vit de taax."

I gave him a five-dollar bill and hoped for the best. With loose change in my pocket, the hot dogs and I retreated back to the mayhem of my office.

The clock was ticking. I devoured both tender morsels in a snap. Then I began to return telephone calls. In between I scanned the day's mail.

A half hour and five phone calls later, it started. At first it was just blurry addresses on the envelopes. But then it was the room. My office had been stationary for as long as I could remember. Now it was spinning. My stomach chimed in. Then I began to sweat profusely as my heart raced. Soon a pain that would immobilize me started to spread through my muscles.

"Are you O.K.?" Cathy asked as she passed my office.

"No," I confirmed, as I sat drenched in sweat.

"What on earth's the matter with you?"

"I'm not sure, but I think I better lie down, before I fall down." I tried to move, but was, for the first time in my life, unable to do so. I slumped involuntarily into a pile on the floor.

Soon I was surrounded by my caring and concerned office staff: law partners, paralegals, secretaries, and a receptionist. They strained for a glimpse of my listless body. People were speaking, but I couldn't match a voice to a face.

"Is he dead?"

"No, he's still sweating. Should we adjust the thermostat?"

"We better call 911."

"Is he supposed to twitch like that?"

"He landed on the Johnston files. Let's move 'em before they're ruined."

"Does anyone know CPR?"

"Did he sign the payroll checks?"

"We better call 911."

"Shouldn't we tell the two on hold that he'll call them back?"

"What's up with his will?"

"Mom always said to wear clean underwear. You think he's wearing..."

"We better call 911."

- - - - - - - - - - - - - - - - - - -

"Mr. Fox?"

A new voice.

"Mr. Fox...are you able to open your eyes?"

I did. But not for long. The room was still spinning.

"Sir, what is your name?"

"His name is Lawrence Fox, middle initial 'B' as in 'Bravo.'"

It was my law partner, Harry.

"Counsellor, I don't want *you* to answer. I want your partner on the floor to."

"I'm so sorry. Ask him again. He answers to 'Larry'."

"Larry, can you sit up?"

Honestly. If I could sit up...if I could talk...would I be on the damn floor?

"Cleo..."

"Yes..."

"Can we get a stretcher through that narrow hallway?"

"I don't think so, Sarg, especially with that sharp right turn."

"Right. Get the drag bag."

The drag bag! I came in today vertically, under my own power. Now I was going out in a bag!

"Larry...can you hear me?"

I opened one eye. A policeman and an ambulance attendant hovered over me.

"We're going to roll you over on your left. Understand?"

What if I didn't?

"Wait Cleo...I think there's a file stuck to his ass."

"Can you get the bag under his hip?"

"Just try to grab his shoulder. O.K.?"

All this time, I had felt the unmistakable hand of death reaching for my body. I now understood how those people in all those old hospital movies just knew when they were going to bite it. Death was less than five minutes away. I began to search for the white light.

"MR. FOX, WE'VE GOT TO STRAP YOU IN. WE DON'T WANT YOU FALLING OUT..."

Oh my God! They were using nursing home speak!

"MR. FOX, ARE YOU STILL THERE?"

They sensed I was about to leave them. So this was it. This was how I would make my grand exit - out the back door in a bag. Great. Course, one-inch thick restraining cords had been fastened securely across my shoulders, stomach and legs. My hands had somehow been rendered immobile as well.

"HOW MUCH DO YOU WEIGH, SIR?"

"Maybe 150 pounds," my law partner interjected again.

"Counsellor. Please!"

"So sorry. I won't say another word," the scolded Harry promised.

The guy in charge put his crotch in my face as he straddled the leather hammock.

"O.K. Cleo, on my count...one...two...three..."

In an instant I was floating in a leather pouch, no doubt toward certain death. Who would have thought I'd go like this? So humiliating.

"Cleo, hoist him up. His ass is dragging on the floor!"

"Sorry boss."

"Now turn the body sideways - there's a sharp bend back here."

The body. I was the body. They knew I was about to die.

"O.K, the guy with all the answers just opened the back door. We can head toward the ambulance, Cleo."

They were about to load my body. I couldn't even wave a last goodbye to my comrades huddled at the back door. (And by the way, just who was answering the phones?) Next time I'd see these folks would be at the cemetery. Life was so short, so unpredictable. Two seductive hot dogs, that's all it took. I should have gone with the energy bars.

That's when I heard the squeal of brakes and smelled burning rubber. A man in a suit had parked his Lexus next to the waiting ambulance. The suit sprinted over to the crowd of office well-wishers, some of whom were by now carrying hankies to wipe away their tears.

"Where's Attorney Fox?" he demanded. Cleo and Sarg paid no attention to the uninvited interloper.

"O.K. Cleo, let's swing him in."

I mustered up a last ounce of strength as a man barely alive.

"Wait...a...minute, Sarg," I groaned.

"Huh?" a confused Sarg asked as he looked about.

"The body. I think the body spoke," Cleo suggested.

"Fox, are you with us?"

"Sarg, hang on....I'm going to....throw up!"

"Thanks for the heads up, counsellor. O.K. Cleo, flip 'em!"

With that, the body snatchers deftly spun me downward in a swift, single move. I now faced the ground, still fastened within the leather drag bag. Ironically, I felt like a piece of pork on a rotisserie spit.

"O.K. You can barf, Fox," Cleo directed.

Then came a startling voice from my left.

"Are you Fox? They said you were Fox. I'm Edgar Hormly. You're a tough guy to get a hold of. Listen, I'm glad I caught you."

"Huh? What the?"

And it was at that moment the digestive gears within me locked, then reversed, sending a day's worth of mini-mart nourishment onto Cleo's feet.

Hormly adroitly jumped aside. "Listen, counsellor, I see you're busy, but I gotta ask a favor. See, if I can get on your calendar for settlement by the 30th, I can save $14.82 in interest on the payoff of my mortgage."

A second torrent exited my body with such energy it would have registered with scientists at a jet propulsion lab.

In an instant, I could feel the hand of death loosen its grip around my throat as I was flipped right side up. The sun was shining and birds were chirping. For the time being, I had escaped the call of the Reaper, and so I wouldn't be joining Harold the ghost and his other friends reclining by day in the upstairs window.

Hormly stood nonplused at the scene of the volcanic vomiting and casually slid out his electronic organizer.

"So...What do you say, counsellor. Can you fit me in by the 30th?"

Chapter 17
The Body Bag

CHAPTER 18

THE FORTUNE TELLER

If everyone had a crystal ball, there would be very little need for lawyers. That's because lawyers are paid to peer into the future in order to help a client avoid a pitfall before it becomes a problem. Lawyers are expected to tell clients to buy enough insurance so that when the house burns down, there is more than just a pile of ashes. Lawyers are called upon to write wills with special clauses and contingencies, so that the dearly departed's untested wishes will be honored, even though the date of death is unknown, and the decedent's children may have spawned five more unforeseen grandchildren. Lawyers draft pre-nuptial contracts so that down the road, when the blessed union turns into a raging fistfight, assets will magically be protected as if no marriage had occurred.

In so many ways, my job as legal counsel is similar to Madame LaRue, the fortuneteller on Fourth and Broad. I have represented her for years. I did her will, and in exchange she told me my fortune. Now that I actually know what's going to happen to me, I won't need a will of my own just yet. LaRue looked at my outstretched palm, then stared into her crystal ball, and told me I am going to be around for a long, long time. But can she actually be trusted to foresee these things? Last week she left her office to get a sandwich. As she was crossing the street, she got hit by a bus and died. Shouldn't she have seen that coming?

Most people never see the approaching bus - even when it's blaring its horn. No. It's usually post problemo that I get the call. Can you blame these folks? I mean, who wants to worry about things in advance? Isn't that a waste of energy? In many ways I envy such people. I, too, would like to stick my head in the sand, and pretend nothing is lurking over the horizon. But instead, I toil day in and day out listening for that horn.

Take Harold, for instance. He's my office pest control guy. Once a month I dutifully pay him to show up and snoop around for mice, flying ants, and other nasty things. My grandparents lived together for 53 years. Toward the end, they started looking like each other. Same with Harold. He's been tracking little critters for so long, he's developed small antennae in his hair, and a nose that twitches like a field mouse.

"You got termites," he announced, as he pointed toward my basement stairs.

Why hadn't Madame LaRue warned me? I would have treated it months ago.

"Now what?" I whined to Harold.

"Not to worry. I'll just pump some sodium triathelate into the beam, and them termites'll be history."

"You can kill them all, guaranteed?"

"Not quite. The good 'ol days is gone forever. The government don't permit the good stuff no more, for so-called 'environmental' reasons. I guess they don't want little kids eating the chemicals nor them poisoned termite carcasses. Or maybe Uncle Sam thinks termites is an endangered species. At any rate, we's only allowed to use stuff that just makes them and children sick, so after that, they'll choose to move away."

"The children?"

"No, the termites."

"The termites? Well, where do they go?"

"Does it matter?"

I told Harold to apply the treatment. Chemicals or no chemicals, termites weren't about to attack my property. He did as instructed and injected sodium triathelate into the wooden beams in my basement. He handed me a written certification that my office had been treated and saved.

Three weeks later, I glanced out the window at my neighbor's residence. Harold had just pulled up in his termite truck. Apparently, there was similar infestation next door.

- - - - - - - - - - - - - - - - - - - -

With all due respect to Mrs. Zeppenfelt, she really should have foreseen this little problem headed her way. Why did she wait so long to call? She reluctantly pushed the official-looking envelope across the conference room table in my direction.

I had been representing Marthanna for 20 years. Once when a discount store attempted to ignore the two year warranty on her malfunctioning stove, I helped her to get a new one. And after her husband Donald died about 10 years ago, I reviewed the real estate contract before she moved into her new mobile home. Because of her limited assets, she purchased the new residence on an installment plan.

The letter from the Social Security Administration began on an up note: "Dear Benefits Recipient." Things went downhill after that.

A tear welled up in Marthanna's eye. "I only got $713 in savings. I don't know if I can pay them back right away."

"Mrs. Zeppenfelt, is any of this true?" I questioned.

"I guess. I mean, maybe. I'm not sure."

I decided to review the letter a second time, since I had never read anything quite like it before. The envelope was addressed to Marthanna's deceased husband:

Dear Benefits Recipient:

An audit of your account has determined that you may no longer be alive. You or your estate maintain the obligation to advise this office when you have died. Funds derived from monthly social security checks negotiated and deposited since the date of your death must be returned forthwith by certified or cashier's check. A computation of monies due follows:

127 monthly payments since date of death at $578.00 per month x 18% compounded interest = total due of $294,088.42. Per diem interest after date of this letter - $76.44.

Very truly yours...

"Shouldn't the funeral home have taken care of this?" Marthanna hypothesized. "I figured if the government sent me the checks, it was O.K. I don't think I could have made ends meet without the money. Does this mean I won't get any more?"

Which question did she want me to answer first?

"I guess I might be able to pay them back possibly 40 or 50 dollars a month, if I don't play bingo each Wednesday," Zeppenfelt proposed. "But it isn't fair, really. After all, they sent me the money. I didn't ask for it."

For a moment I could see clearly into the future. Marthanna's bingo evenings were about to end, unless of course, bingo is played in the federal penitentiary.

Chapter 18
The Fortune Teller

CHAPTER 19

THE ACTUARIAL COMPUTATION

In Pennsylvania, if someone's death is caused by the negligence of another, both the decedent's estate and those the decedent left behind may possess separate causes of action to sue the wrongdoer. It has always intrigued me that such legal proceedings could not have been named more illogically.

A "survival action" is brought in the name of the dead guy who *didn't* survive, while a "wrongful death action" is initiated by the grieving *survivors.* So much for common sense.

Loomis and Hapalona Cudlip were waiting in my office conference room. They had called to talk about an issue "involving a baby." That's all my secretary could recall. At first glance they appeared to be normal, had all their teeth, and both were dressed as if they were off to church. I decided to take the plunge.

"Good afternoon. I'm Larry Fox."

Loomis stuck out his hand and introduced his wife. A polite mid-30s couple.

"You folks from around here?"

"We live over in Kesslersville," Loomis confirmed.

"That's a nice town. What do you do for a living?"

"I'm an accountant. Hapalona here sells venetian blinds." She shook her head up and down to assure me that her mate was telling the truth.

"Tell me, how might I help you?"

"Well, it's like this," Loomis began. "We've got two kids already."

"Been married eight years," Hapalona interjected.

"Eight years," Loomis repeated. "So last year, I had a vasectomy and Happy had her tubes tied. Two kids are enough."

Belt and suspenders, I thought to myself. He really *is* an accountant.

"And then, last month, I learned I was pregnant again," Hapalona announced. "I guess his sperm can find their way anywhere."

"Look," he explained, "it wasn't that much fun, my little visit to Dr. Tweedly. He tells me to hop up on the table, and the next thing I know this enclave of student nurses, or maybe it was a Brownie troop - I can't be sure - gathers around, watching my unmentionables dangling in the breeze. Snip, snip, nothing to it, he explains. Well, for the next three days I was walking a little funny since my private parts swelled up like grapefruits. For that type of misery, I expect to be shooting blanks, just as promised."

"I had my tubes tied," Mrs. Cudlip chimed in. "Then a year after our operations, he goes and knocks me up!"

Either this duo was the nuttiest couple to ever wander into my office, or they were the most fertile. I wondered if I should congratulate them on their future arrival. Loomis beat me to the punch.

"Here's the thing," he proclaimed. "I know you can sue in Pennsylvania for wrongful death."

"Yes," I tentatively agreed as I tried to follow where he was going with this.

"Well, we want to sue for wrongful life."

She nodded up and down again.

Had I heard him correctly? "Wrongful life!"

"Through that doctor's negligence, there's gonna be another mouth to feed, another body to clothe, and another brain to educate," he said matter-of-factly.

Was this guy expecting triplets?

"And it isn't my fault, no sireee."

Logistically thinking, I didn't necessarily agree with that last statement.

"Are you listening to us?" the bean counter questioned.

"Huh? Oh, yes. There isn't any."

"Any what?"

"Wrongful life. Just think, a couple more kids, and you can start your own bowling league." This attempt at stand-up comedy, as usual, fell completely flat.

"We want to sue," Loomis persisted.

I had to hear this.

"For what, exactly?"

"Now that's more like it."

Loomis reached into his suit jacket pocket, and pulled out a small notebook and a portable calculator.

"It's all here actuarially in black and white. You'll note I'm not seeking any medical reimbursement, since we have full health coverage."

He turned the computations in my direction.

Clothing...18 years...$34,380

"You dress this child rather well," I noted.

"Only the best for our kids." Hapalona nodded.

Food...18 years...$77,096

"It's a high-protein diet," Loomis confirmed.

Education...22 years...$385,540

"Private school, of course. The last four years will be at Princeton. She'll have to pay for any graduate degree herself."

I added the numbers on my tablet. "You want $497,016 in damages?"

"Plus interest. I could have put all that money in the bank. If the doctor hedges, I'll ask for the cost of summer camp, baby-sitters, piano lessons, and vacations, too."

They had come here for advice, and I had some. She ought to go back on the pill, and he should start using condoms, and with their history, even that might not be enough.

"Mr. and Mrs. Cudlip," I began, "I don't think I can help you. You can't sue because you're having a baby. Having a child is a blessing. Some people hope in vain to have such a dream come true. You should give thanks for your good fortune and never look back."

Loomis stood up.

"If you won't help us, I guess we'll find a more forward- thinking lawyer."

Mrs. Cudlip nodded her head. Then we shook hands and they left.

- - - - - - - - - - - - - - - - - - - -

About a year later, I received a letter. It was from the Cudlips.

Dear Attorney Fox:

Melissa was born three months ago. We enclose a picture. She is a blessing from God, as are our other children. Thanks for the advice.

Very truly yours,

Loomis and Happy

I carefully studied the snapshot of the new arrival. Loomis was right. She probably would attend Princeton.

Chapter 19
The Acturial Computation

CHAPTER 20

PROFESSOR THOMPSON MAKES A POINT

Professor Icabod Thompson taught torts, future interests, and real property at Villanova Law School. He knew more about torts than any 20 professional slip-and-fall con artists combined. Until I met him, I had never heard of the word "tort." I didn't know that torts lurked everywhere, and could occur at the drop of a hat.

The professor successfully avoided a vast array of torts that might have personally afflicted him. That's because he employed a chauffeur to drive his black Mercedes sedan. This uniformed employee kept the car in immaculate condition, washing and polishing it daily.

During my first week of studies, I happened to be standing alone near the rear entrance of the law school. From this vantage point, you could see the entire faculty parking lot. It was then that a shadowy figure with bands of long, unkempt hair approached me.

"These cars are owned by the professors," he volunteered. "I'm Elijah."

"I'm Larry," I tentatively responded.

"Are you sure your name isn't Ishmael?"

"Quite certain."

"No matter. Larry, when the first snow falls, all those cars shall disappear, save one," the gaunt figure said with a wave of his hand.

He made a slight bow, and withdrew down the hall. I never saw him again.

Just before the Christmas break, the first snow fell. Soon, every car was covered in white, with the exception of Thompson's black Mercedes. It was polished to such a degree that any snowflake that had the audacity to land on it quickly slipped off.

The professor taught us that tortious activity could be avoided if one acted in a "reasonable" manner.

"The law seeks out *The Reasonable Man* and it is his behavior that is used as the standard in determining if someone has acted inappropriately," Thompson explained from his pulpit at the front of the gloomy lecture hall. The bleak mood had not been set by the professor. Rather, it had been raining off and on for the better part of a month. It was drizzling again as we sat taking notes.

The front of the classroom was accentuated by a large prominent polished gold crucifix. Each classroom contained the same religious symbol, for this institution had been founded by monks affiliated with the Order Of St. Augustine. Professor Thompson took two steps backward and stood immediately below the two-foot metal cross. With arms outstretched, he posed a rhetorical question.

"Who then is the Reasonable Man?"

For an instant, the dark clouds outside parted, and a narrow beam of sunlight, unseen for nearly a month, streamed into the lecture hall and landed upon the crucifix, causing a temporary golden glow to encircle Thompson's head. He then stepped forward, and the beam of light vanished. The entire enlightenment had taken less than five seconds.

Professor Thompson also lectured about future interests. Until I attended his class, I had no idea someone could claim a legal interest in the future. The professor introduced me to the concept of fee tails, remainder interests with life estates, and devises by special warranty. Our 720 page textbook was entitled *The Rule Against Perpetuities*. This massive treatise contained 204 appellate cases spanning 600 years of British and colonial law regarding the Rule Against Perpetuities. There was only one thing missing - the Rule. Nowhere in this two and one-half pound book was there the specific language that quoted the Rule verbatim. All I could gather from a reading of the caselaw was that the Rule had been enacted to discourage the creation of perpetuities. So here is my best guess, after three years of law school and more than 30 years of practice in the law as to the wording of this elusive rule: "Don't create any perpetuities."

There was one other problem: what is a perpetuity? Here's what I was able to decipher from the six centuries of caselaw: If something goes on too long (like a 720 page textbook) it's a perpetuity, and ought to be banned.

Professor Thompson peered out above his cut-away bifocals and squinted at the throng of eager students assembled before him.

"Now suppose, class, that Mr. Landowner owns a 200 acre estate. In his last will and testament, he devises the estate to his son, to be used by his son during the lifetime of the son. When the son dies, the estate is to go to the son's son during the lifetime of the son's son. Thereafter, the estate is to go to the son of the son's son during the lifetime of the son of the son's son. And so on for eight more generations. As a result, Mr. Landowner will be able to rule from the grave for at least four or five hundred years. Is this legal?"

Some bright scholar sitting beside of me raised his hand and was acknowledged by Thompson.

"No, Professor. Such a last will and testament violates the Rule against Perpetuities. No devise of real estate can exceed a life in being plus 21 years."

"Correct," Thompson agreed. "A devise exceeding a life in being plus 21 years creates a perpetuity, which the rule precludes."

Apparently it was illegal to devise your house to the next seven or eight generations of your children's children. One's interest in the future had its limits. Thompson's wisdom, on the other hand, seemed boundless. Surprisingly, it was outside the classroom that I first noted this fact.

I had been invited to a freshman-faculty tea in the law school lounge, where staff and student might meet informally. Thompson was there, accompanied by his wife, Lucinda. They were both in their mid-70s, and both appeared healthy and content. But what caught my attention was the way they looked at each other, as if no one else was in the room.   These folks were in love.   Were they newlyweds?

"Hah!" Thompson scoffed.   My inquiry made Mrs. Thompson laugh as well.

"It will be 52 years next September that I've been married to the same woman," the professor noted.   "This woman," he pointed.

"September 8th," Lucinda chimed in.

"Over half a century!" I marveled.   "Tell me, Professor, is there a secret to a long and loving marriage?"

Icabod thought for a moment about the last five decades, and then he gave me some advice I'd carry with me for a lifetime.

"I'll let you in on a little secret, young man."   He lowered his voice.

"When my bride and I became engaged, we took a solemn oath.   It was agreed that I, alone, would make all decisions regarding any *major* issues that might affect the marriage.   We also agreed that Lucinda would make all decisions regarding any *minor* issues."

"And this system has worked?"

"Yes.   What is surprising to me, however, is the fact that in 52 years, there hasn't been a single major decision for me to make."

- - - - - - - - - - - - - - - - - - -

Indeed, philosophers have been struggling with the concept of "love" well before Plato wrote his discourses. From the male perspective one cynical comic has said that love is the delusion that any two women are different from each other.

It is possible to quarrel, and yet continue to be in love.   My friend Hubert is a man of very few words.   His wife, Ethel, didn't know they were having one of their fights for two weeks. He finally had to tell her, so they could make up.

Actually, there are several different forms of love. Some are easier to describe than others. A partial list includes the immutable affection a mother has for her child. It is unconditional, and is incapable of dissolution. If the child ends up a mass murderer on death row, Mom will still show up at the prison on visiting day.

There is the love one spouse has for another. It can be quite strong, but it can be altered in an instant. As an example, the admission "but I only slept with her once last month," can bring about an instant change in the relationship.

Perhaps the strangest form of love is that found at the corner tavern. Two drunks sitting on neighboring bar stools will buy each other drinks all night, sharing their limited resources until each passes out.

There is another form of love, and it may be limitless. I unexpectedly discovered it hidden in a remote office of the county courthouse.

I had just sat through an hour of arraignment court with more than 100 defendants and about 20 attorneys. The judge finally called a recess, and so we all poured out of the double doors, free at last. I said my good-byes to both the shoplifter and the swindler I represented, reminding them to show up on time for their next hearings. Then I began the familiar journey from Courtroom One down the hall to the Recorder of Deeds office. The usual collection of misfits loitered in the hallway, some talking with their legal counsel, others mumbling among themselves. Some greaseball sporting an oversized gold earring and a ponytail clasped his hands above his protruding potbelly.

"These stinkin' lawyers - they're all legalized bloodsuckers. We get caught, they get paid. If it weren't for us, they'd be broke."

The guy with "mom" tattooed on his upper arm agreed. And thank goodness he had a close relationship with at least one parent. Where he was going, he'd need it on visiting days.

"Yeah," he nodded. "Without us criminals, them lawyers would be sunk, and so would those courthouse workers. We keep the whole system operational."

His logic was impeccable, similar to the lady who smashed into my car from behind while I was stopped at a red light.

"That damn lawyer was in my way," she explained to the cop.

Did everyone view lawyers and those who worked in the system as cold-blooded snakes?

I made my way to the Recorder of Deeds office. I had 15 minutes left to file a mortgage before heading back to the office to squeeze in my next client interview. I ran into Andrew Ogilvie. He had been practicing law nearly as long as I had. We both pursued similar small office practices. No front-page clients. Just long hours, deadlines to meet, and never-ending overhead.

I hadn't seen him in three or four months. He wasn't right. He looked tired. His face was ashen in color. His steps were halting, and his breathing seemed shallow.

"You O.K. Andrew?" I asked.

"As well as can be expected," he said with the shrug of his shoulders that now seemed too small for his jacket. He recorded a deed at the counter, waved to me, and headed toward the door.

Two weeks later, I again made the journey to the Recorder's office. One of the secretaries' eyes welled up as she talked on the phone at her desk. She turned to the clerk seated next to her.

"Thank God. They're both O.K."

The clerk burst into tears of joy. Word spread rapidly throughout the office. Title searchers, settlement clerks, and other staff working in the large room all gave thanks in various ways. Brenda, the copy machine operator, was the first to approach me.

"Great news about Andrew and Melissa, huh? They're critical now, but still, what a blessing, right?"

"Forgive me," I confessed. "I - "

132

"You haven't heard?"

"No."

"Andrew Ogilvie has been on the transplant list for a new kidney for almost a year. His condition got real bad a couple of months ago. You know Melissa? The assistant supervisor here? Well, she knew about it and had herself tested to see if she'd be a compatible donor. She was, so this week she went to Philadelphia, where Andrew received one of her kidneys."

"How are they related?"

"They're not. She met him here. The courthouse. But she said he was a nice guy."

Chapter 20
Professor Thompson Makes A Point

CHAPTER 21

THE OTHER SIDE OF THE STORY

Internet information is boundless. As a result, privacy is hardly considered sacred. Data once stored in dusty vaults at the Northampton County Courthouse are now retrievable at the touch of a button. My next door neighbor can log on and see whether I have paid my real estate taxes, if I have been sued lately, what value the assessment office has placed upon my residence, which bank holds my mortgage, whether my payments are current, and how many toilets exist on my first floor. I can find out if my neighbor has voted recently, whether his dog has received its timely rabies shot, when he was last charged with a crime, and how his mother died. Copies of her autopsy report are available for $5.00.

Is universal access a good thing?

- - - - - - - - - - - - - - - - - - - -

Johnson and Chrysanthemum Wigfall had been married for eight years. She must have loved him, or at least thought she did at some point. Whatever the case, she took his name and together they produced two children - ages seven and five. It was a good life, or should have been. He worked as vice-president of some hi-tech corporation out in the industrial park. His inflated salary permitted her to stay home and raise the kids. Saturdays and Sundays he played golf at the country club. She didn't care for the sport, so she usually took the children to their never ending dance, piano, and art lessons. Sundays they went to church without him. They appeared to be the perfect family. The bills were paid; the offspring weren't sick; money had already been set aside for future orthodontic costs; and there was food on the table that graced the oversized kitchen of the 12-room house located in the town's trendiest neighborhood.

Yet there she sat in my office, seeking a divorce. She was emotionless, and began to talk to the wall, as if I weren't in the room.

"Eight years of marriage. All he does is watch sports on TV. On the weekends, he plays golf."

A week later, I agreed to meet with Mr. Wigfall's attorney, Lorenzo Livingood in the company of our respective clients, to see if we could amicably work out the initial game plan. Did Mr. Wigfall intend to move out of the home? Would Chrysanthemum get custody of the kids? How much support would he agree to pay? If he kept the BMW, would she retain the van?

We gathered in my conference room. Johnson Wigfall sat bolt upright, his lips in a grimace. There was a question or two on his mind.

"Chrissy, just why the hell are you leaving me?"

Chrysanthemum just stared straight ahead, as if no question had been asked.

"What did I do wrong?" her soon to be ex-husband implored. "Did I ever beat you, whore around, refuse to go to work, fail to pay the bills, or neglect my duties as a father?"

There was a long silence.

"No," my client replied softly.

"Then I just don't get it," Johnson huffed. "I don't get it."

I tried to steer the conversation toward the ground rules for support and visitation, but Mr. Wigfall would have none of it.

"We're outta here," he announced to Lorenzo. "She's insane." He stood up and left the room.

His attorney shook my hand. "I'll call you in a couple of days," he promised.

Was the house big enough until next week?

There are two types of divorce clients: Those who find no need to relate their life story, and those who -

"When I was a little girl, I always wanted a Chihuahua," Chrysanthemum began.

I sat back down.

"You know, the little type of dog," she explained as she made a cradling motion with her arms.

"Yes," I assured her.

"I don't know why, but I've always wanted one, to hold and pet. Never had one. I asked Johnson, but he's allergic or something. No cats. No dogs."

"That's unfortunate."

"I even prayed at church for one. Johnson used to go to church with me, but then he stopped. He's not a bad man, mind you. Like he said, he's never hit me."

"I'm glad to hear that."

"He works hard. In two years, the mortgage will be paid off. But each night when he comes home, he doesn't seem to have any time for me or the kids. He has some beers, smokes a cigar, eats some pretzels, and watches sports on TV. Football is his favorite, but he likes basketball and hockey and baseball and bowling, too. He tapes all the games he misses, so he can watch them later. Do you watch sports?"

"No."

"Neither do I. So each night I spend my time e-mailing my twin sister who still lives in Detroit, and we talk. I miss her."

"That's understandable."

"We talk a lot. Sometimes Johnson takes me and the kids to the country club. Do you know how I can tell who is married and who isn't?"

"No."

"The married couples don't talk to each other. Maybe a little with their kids, but they don't speak to each other. Single people on dates, now *they* talk!" She smiled for the first time.

"Johnson doesn't talk ... to me. He carries on a pretty good conversation with the TV when he watches football and golf with his beer and pretzels and cigar. My kids are beginning to watch football and eat pretzels, too. I don't think either one of them has ever held a Chihuahua, though. Have you ever held one?"

"Yes. They're cute."

"Can I tell you something?"

"Sure."

"A couple of months ago I couldn't sleep. It was three in the morning. Johnson was snoring down the hallway in the recliner in front of the TV. I was about to e-mail my sister, but instead, I decided to surf the Internet. Know what I found?"

"No."

· "In .Detroit near where my sister lives, they have a local chapter of the Chihuahua Club of America. There's a website and a chat room. Soon I was talking to this guy Howard, at 3:00 in the morning. He just had a litter of Chihuahuas. They were all doing well, including the mother. We just talked about Chihuahuas. That's all. And then I looked out the window and it was daybreak. We had been gabbing non-stop for three solid hours.

"Well, the next couple of early mornings, we met in the chat room again. Then I got out my platinum credit card, and told Johnson I was going to visit my sister in Detroit for a few days. Howard met me at the airport. He brought a Chihuahua! I would've spotted him anywhere. He's bald, and walks with a cane. When you finally find your soul mate, these little things don't matter. I'm no prize, either.

"We spent the weekend with his 12 Chihuahuas. He doesn't smoke cigars, eat pretzels or watch sports. Why his wife left him I'll never know. Guess where we went? The dog shelter. We had a ball. And when he touched my hand, I felt it, you know? Like it was meant to be. I never felt that before. And you know something?..."

"What's that, Mrs. Wigfall?"

"If Johnson had just once shown 15 minutes of interest in Chihuahuas, I'd probably have stayed the next 15 years, for the sake of the kids. But I'm done. Draw up the papers."

Ferdy Krothammel is my plumber. My law office is housed in a 150-year-old Georgian style building. At one time, it was a funeral home. Before that, it may have been some bank president's mansion. One thing is certain - every pipe leading to every toilet, sink, and drain has been replaced - or will be - usually on an emergency basis. As a result, Ferdy has become an important part of my life. When his wife suddenly left him, I unhesitatingly agreed to represent him in his divorce.

Webster's Dictionary defines a "pessimist" as a person who habitually sees or anticipates the worst, or is disposed to be gloomy. An "optimist," on the other hand, is a person who is disposed to look on the more favorable side of happenings and to anticipate the most favorable result.

Of course, these definitions are backward. It is the optimist whose life is filled with gloom and the pessimist who's often pleasantly surprised.

Take Ferdy, for example. Until recently, he had been living with his wife for 18 years. That's 6,570 days give or take. They fought every single day. She always prevailed. Yet without fail, the next morning, Ferdy would wake up again, and optimistically think this might be the day he would finally win his first argument. His hopes were soon dashed.

"She left me last Wednesday," he announced, as he cocked his head to the left. "By the way, is that a drip?"

"I hope not. Did you know she was thinking of splitting up?" I asked.

"Nope. But she's been acting funny lately. When I watch back-to-back football games plus the highlights, she gets on the Internet. I don't know what the hell she does for hours on end in front of that stupid screen."

Chapter 21
The Other Side Of The Story

CHAPTER 22

GLINDA

There can be no property rights without law, and there can be no law without property rights.

My favorite movie deals with disputed property rights regarding a pair of slippers. Different parties claim to maintain divergent interests in the coveted ruby-encrusted footwear, which is removed from a corpse without permission from the estate of the decedent. Thereafter, the priceless pumps are used to magically transport the new owner back to the Midwest without a plane ticket.

The shoes are purloined with the assistance of a co-conspirator with an egocentric belief that good witches are beautiful, and bad witches are ugly, and therefore the latter deserve to have their footwear stolen even before the body is cold. I do love a complex plot. Don't you?

Anyway, the beautiful, egocentric witch doesn't need a plane ticket either. She arrives in a silver bubble that initially appears as a dot over the horizon and grows to the size of a weather balloon. Finally, she descends without flight clearance within a few yards of the decedent, who was killed when a house mysteriously fell on her near a colony of munchkins. The beautiful witch isn't upset that the decedent is lying, at best, near death, and helpless. She doesn't offer to perform CPR. She doesn't call for a doctor. Rather, she gives the protagonist of the movie misleading directions regarding the location of a city wherein resides a wizard who theoretically might assist in returning the heroine to her home, all of which is unnecessary, since the beautiful witch knows it is possible to transport individuals to foreign places merely by clicking the shoes together - a secret she doesn't divulge until the end of the picture.

Actually, the wizard turns out to be a fraud, since he tries to give people heart and brain transplants, even though he doesn't have a license to practice medicine. Need I go on?

- - - - - - - - - - - - - - - - - - -

Here's a call I'll never forget. This one came less than an hour after a surprise cold front slammed into the Valley. It was so powerful it uprooted some trees and knocked out a few power lines.

"Mr. Fox?"

"Yes."

"Officer Crenshaw. Airport Security."

Those airport rent-a-cops. Dick Tracy wanna-bes, with their short, staccato phrases.

"How can I help you?"

"It's your plane, Sir. Hangar 12."

"What about it?"

"Tornado, Sir. You better come quick."

Tornado? This isn't Kansas! I couldn't recall a tornado ever touching down in eastern Pennsylvania. I pressed for more information.

"It was a mini-twister. Touched down here at the airport, Sir. It demolished your hangar. Then it left the area."

"But my plane was in that hangar!"

"Not any more, Sir."

I rushed to the airport. It was only 3:00 p.m., yet it might as well have been midnight. Black thunderclouds hid the sun, turning day into night. Menacing rain clouds swirled overhead, as 45 mph winds swept through the area. Once in a while, a lightning bolt would strike the ground - proof of the passing storm's intensity.

The 30 private hangars stood in neat rows, like small hunting cabins bordering a lake. Each had been similarly constructed in the shape of the letter *T*. I instinctively headed in the direction of my hangar, hoping against hope that -

Every hangar was intact, except mine. I stared in disbelief as I slowly exited my car. Only one wall of the structure remained upright. Most of the wooden roof was gone. One entire wing of my plane was missing, as was the tail. The propeller was bent. Two security guards roping off the area approached me.

"We found the ailerons lying on Runway 6. Some of your avionics were located half a mile away near the terminal building."

I stood in the drenching rain, unable to move, unable to speak. This was no way for a retractable-gear aristocrat to die, without so much as a final flight together. We had shared so many adventures.

I thought back to the first day of the air traffic controllers' strike. Ronald Reagan had just been elected. Miss Mooney, as I called her, and I departed from Oshkosh, Wisconsin, and had received a clearance to cruising altitude on an instrument flight routing back to Pennsylvania. I was pilot in command with three other souls on board. I called into Cleveland approach to request a change in altitude since we were in the clouds and were hitting some turbulence.

"Mooney 7887 November, this is Cleveland approach. We're about to go on strike this morning, so you're on your own. Good luck."

Miss Mooney knew we were in trouble, but she didn't skip a beat. Soon some supervisor in New York, still monitoring the radio waves, took pity on us, and guided us back to safety.

As I gazed upon the wreckage, wiping the pelting rain from my eyes, I thought I saw a small aircraft light approaching over South Mountain, perhaps 10 nautical miles to the south. Was it possible some fool was flying around in the remnants of this storm? The light grew bigger. Soon it was hovering over the airport. Then a spotlight beamed directly on me. The helicopter descended and landed about 300 feet from my destroyed hangar. The whirling blades finally came to rest. I read the bright yellow wording that spanned the length of the uninvited craft: *Chopper 6 - Action News.*

But wait. This was *my* private wake, my special moment of closure with the mortally wounded Miss Mooney. I would not suffer interlopers during this, my last good-bye.

The helicopter door popped open. A hidden folding staircase tumbled to the ground. And then I saw her familiar striking face. In gusting wind, her hair was motionless. In driving rain, her make-up remained streak-free. The dress? A designer original. The body? Sculpted by a plastic surgeon and a private trainer. A cameraman emerged just in time to position an umbrella over her head. She approached as I stood soaked and in mourning over the loss of my tangled friend.

She stuck a microphone in my face. The cameraman turned on a portable light to capture the moment. "That your plane?"

I remained silent.

"Hi, I'm Glinda."

I knew that. I knew from my favorite old movie that once in a while a beautiful witch will drop in unannounced, to look great, but offer zero help.

"Go away."

She inched the microphone a little closer.

"How do you feel about the mess that tornado made of your plane? Isn't it something how it hit just *your* hangar! Of all the luck!"

My parents had always taught me to be polite. This was to be the exception to the rule.

"Get the *#@% outta here!"

She backed off and started filming what was left of the hangar.

That night I got a call from my old law school roommate who had set up a practice in Philadelphia.

"Saw you on the 10 o'clock news."

"You did?"

"Nice to see you're still a man of few words."

Indeed I am. And I can find my way to the Emerald City without directions from Glinda.

Chapter 22
Glinda

CHAPTER 23

THE PUMPING STATION

And so it was decided that the two foes would be divided by the 38th parallel: North Korea on the north; South Korea on the south.

Quote from my 5th grade history book

- - - - - - - - - - - - - - - - - - - -

They were at war with each other, even though no formal written declaration had been promulgated. The line of demarcation was Turtle Gap Road. To the north stretched North Manheim Township. To the south lay South Manheim Township. With the commencement of hostilities, the township's elected supervisors communicated with the enemy camp only by e-mail. How unfortunate, since just two short years earlier, relations had been cordial as the two neighboring townships worked together on everything from leaf collection to civil defense testing.

"It's their fault," Cecic Suck assured me. He was president of the South Manheim Township Board of Supervisors. I served as the Board's solicitor.

Maybe he was right, but who cared? It was senseless that two neighboring political entities in eastern Pennsylvania looked upon each other as enemies.

I had heard it all before, but Cecic apparently thought the story was worth repeating again, even though our formal weekly board meeting had concluded and the hour was late.

"It all started with the big snowfall the season before last. We were prepared and ready to go. Our plow made it all the way up Turtle Gap Road to the very crest of the mountain..."

Even though two feet of snow fell...I mused to myself.

"Even though two feet of snow fell," Cecic confirmed. "But not North Manheim. Did they plow the other side of the crest? Noo-oo. Can you imagine that? Anyway, none of our people coming over the mountain could get home. I filed a complaint. Did they even respond? Noo-oo. Well, I'll tell you what, Fox, what comes around goes around. Get it?"

Yes, I did. He was going to tell me about the leaf collection truck again.

"So guess what happened when their leaf collection truck broke down? You're damn right. I refused to let them borrow ours."

"*What's right is right,*" I heard a voice in my head anticipate.

"What's right is right," Suck lectured.

- - - - - - - - - - - - - - - - - - -

It had taken more than a year and a half, but all of South Manheim Township's hard work had paid off. My client received formal notice from Harrisburg that a grant to fund the expansion of its sewer system had been approved. Capacity of the sewage treatment plant would increase five-fold. Hundreds upon hundreds of new homes could now be constructed, their sewage needs serviced by the municipality.

North Manheim Township had no sewage treatment plant. When news of the new capacity became public, its supervisors sent out an olive branch, a diplomatic letter inquiring if their township might also utilize the new facility.

"Like hell. That'll be the day," Cecic huffed at the weekly board meeting. "They snub us for two years and now they want to kiss and make up? Guess what, friends? Nothin' doin.'"

"Mr. Suck," I interjected.

"What?"

"I respectfully ask you and the other supervisors to reconsider. You could charge a substantial fee for the service. Think of the township budget."

"We know that, counsellor. But why help out North Manheim? Let's keep the new capacity for ourselves. We can build more homes right here."

The other supervisors agreed. My intervention as a peacemaker was unwanted and rejected.

Three months later, a real estate developer bought the old Odenheimer farm, and submitted plans to the township for a 500 home subdivision. The new treatment plant made the proposal feasible, as long as certain conditions were met.

"That tract is predominantly below grade," the Planning Commission advised the developer. "You'll have to pay for the installation of a pumping station."

The developer agreed. A pump house would be constructed to township standards, to push waste products up hill to the treatment plant. The treatment plant engineer drew up the plans, and construction began in early spring. Once the pumping station became operational, erection of the 500 homes would follow.

- - - - - - - - - - - - - - - - - - -

It was Elmo on the phone. "You'd better come over to the municipal building *now*. We have a major problem."

So much for my low cholesterol watercress and cucumber salad.

"I'll be right over. By the way, what's the difficulty?"

"I'll explain when you get here."

In 20 minutes, I was face-to-face with Elmo, the township engineer, the sewage treatment plant manager, and the township construction official.

"See, here's the thing," Elmo began. "The pumping station is up and running as of this week."

"That's good, isn't it?" I suggested.

"It is. But check out this e-mail from North Manheim Township," Bill Gosling, the engineer, interjected. He pushed a piece of paper across the table.

Dear Gentlepeople:

The Board of Supervisors of North Manheim Township notes the presence of a newly constructed sewage pumping station approximately 300 yards from the intersection of Gooseberry Lane and Tumblebrook Court. Our survey finds that this facility has been constructed within the Township of North Manheim on real estate owned by the township without the requisite permit or approvals. Consider this letter formal notice to remove the trespassing structure.

Best regards,

North Manheim Township

I read the letter a second time, then I looked up. "You guys built the pumping station in the wrong township?"

"See, it's like this," Gosling back-pedaled. "That location is real near where the two townships come together at the highway interchange. We always thought that because the traffic light actually takes up most of the room near the two billboards, it was part of our right-of-way, but apparently - "

"Excuse me," I interrupted again. "Did we build in the wrong township?"

"Maybe by about 80 feet," Neal Fromhold, the construction official, admitted.

"On their land?" I repeated.

"It's possible. Our surveyor just did some preliminary work," Elmo explained. "He says it doesn't look good."

"Can it be removed?" I questioned.

"I suppose anything can be relocated," the engineer offered. "But I'd rather try to reposition the Empire State Building."

"Oh? Why?"

"The piping for the sludge runs under the highway, there's electrical conduit everywhere, massive pumps, and enough meters and dials to operate Hoover Dam."

"Don't surveys usually happen *before* construction?"

"Nobody thought it was necessary," the engineer suggested. "The land appeared useless, surrounded by traffic signals."

- - - - - - - - - - - - - - - - - - -

The next morning, I telephoned the president of the North Manheim Township supervisors, Kermit Zoberwickel.

"I've been expecting your call," he laughed.

After the usual pleasantries, I decided to ask a few questions.

"Did we really build on you land?"

"Yup. Your idiot construction guy missed the border by 83 feet. We usually do *our* surveys first."

"When did you realize the mistake?"

"The first day your people stuck a shovel in the ground."

"You didn't say anything."

"Look, pal. If we couldn't have a treatment plant, we'll settle for a pumping station. By the way, it can stay for a buck a year."

"That sounds like a pretty reasonable lease."

"We're reasonable people, as long as we get 1,000 sewer hook-ups. We'll even pay the service fees."

I immediately suggested to my supervisors that they take the deal. They did. After that came shared snowplow and leaf-collection vehicle use. For the first time, the 38th parallel began to fade, as amicable municipal bureaucrats coordinated their efforts. Ultimately 1,000 new toilets were flushing around the clock.

Chapter 23

The Pumping Station

CHAPTER 24

CONFRONTATION AT THE O.K. CORRAL

I have little in common with people who find it necessary to co-habit with exotic beasts. Lions, tigers, and bears belong in the woods, or at the zoo. Every once in a while I'll catch an article about some idiot raising a 20-foot boa constrictor in his bathtub, or a jerk who takes his full-grown alligator for walks in the park. Sometimes there's a follow-up piece in the newspaper with an accompanying photo of the satisfied beasts after they've swallowed their owners whole. I have little sympathy, unless, of course, the snake or crocodile ends up with indigestion or food poisoning.

Mildred Kleppelmyer was breathing heavily on the phone. There was fear in her voice.

"Is something wrong?" I inquired.

"Why do you think I'm calling?" she huffed. "We just received a certified letter from the township zoning guy. He says we're breaking the law. But we're not, because Pickles is a pet, just like a dog or a - "

"Mrs. Kleppelmyer..."

"What?" (sob)

"Who is Pickles?"

"Our horse."

"You own a horse?"

"Yes, Pickles."

"Why is ownership of this horse illegal?"

"That's what I wanted to find out from *you*. I thought you were supposed to know."

"Mildred, what I meant was - why does the zoning officer think your ownership of a horse constitutes a violation of the zoning code?"

"Wait a minute. I'll get the letter ... Here it is. Should I read it to you?"

"Yes."

"O.K."

Dear Mr. and Mrs. Kleppelmyer:

A complaint has been filed with this office alleging that you are presently engaged in the activity of animal husbandry within a residential zoning district. Such activity is only permitted in the agricultural zone. Section 1.04 of the Township of New Saucon zoning ordinance defines 'animal husbandry' as 'the raising and keeping of any kind of livestock, poultry, horse(s), ponies or other large domestic animal(s), or the keeping or raising of any combination of more than four small domestic animals (dogs, cats, pigeons, rabbits, etc.) whether or not as pets.'

You are required to cease and desist from engaging in such activity. Should you object to this determination, you may seek to obtain a variance from the zoning hearing board.

Very truly yours,

Blanco E. Franco,
Zoning Administrator

"Mildred..."

"Yes..."

"Where do you live?"

"4020 Mulberry Lane, in the township."

"In the new subdivision built by Frankel Brothers?"

"Yes. We moved in last year."

The Kleppelmyers resided in an upscale neighborhood. Anyone driving in their neck of the woods would be hard pressed to find laundry hanging out to dry or an aluminum recreational vehicle abandoned among growing weeds in the backyard. This is where the child psychologists and the Internet analysts choose to live. Four-car garages came as standard equipment, because it's such a pain moving the Jaguar to get to the Mercedes.

"Where do you board your horse, Mrs. Kleppelmyer?"

"In the spare bedroom."

"What?"

"Pickles is a *miniature* horse. She's less than two feet high full grown, and weighs less than some dogs."

"Who rides this horse?" I asked.

"Nobody. You wouldn't saddle up a Labrador retriever, would you?"

No, I wouldn't. But I'm not sure I'd have a horse sleeping in the spare bedroom. However, I was intrigued with my client's dilemma. After all, the ordinance only referred to the keeping of *large* domestic animals. Pickles, it could be argued, didn't fall into that category. I had never seen such an animal. I decided an on-site investigation was warranted.

"Sure," Mildred agreed. "Come on over."

That weekend I moseyed on over to the Kleppelmyer spread. This home on the range was indeed impressive, with an expansive circular driveway and a stone mailbox large enough to serve as a guesthouse. This was not where I envisioned encountering a horse.

"Welcome to our home," Mrs. Kleppelmyer said as she greeted me at a front door big enough to drive a stagecoach through. I trotted on in. The massive combination lobby and living room was covered by imported ceramic tile. I didn't notice any horse pies.

"Of course not," Mildred assured me. "For the most part, Pickles is housebroken. If we go away for extended periods, we just attach a diaperbucket."

Why hadn't I thought of that?

"Where is Pickles?" I inquired.

"She's finishing up lunch in the kitchen. I'll introduce you."

I followed her past the vast dining room into a cavernous kitchen, the type designed for small parties of less than 60. There was a horse the size of a St. Bernard. It was eating some grain out of a mixing bowl that could have been used to feed the 7th cavalry. A little water trough engraved with the name "Pickles" was positioned against a wall near one of the refrigerators. Every once in a while, the animal's hooves would make a clicking sound as it repositioned itself on the floor's Greek marble tiles.

"Pickles?" I exclaimed.

"Neigh," she answered.

I was sold.

I filed an application for a variance, seeking an interpretation as to whether the zoning ordinance was applicable to this type of lovable pet. Kleppelmyers' surrounding neighbors received notice of the public hearing. This would expose the hidden enemy, for I didn't know who had initially complained to the zoning official.

I prepared for Pickles' big day in court. I read every article I could find on miniature horses, domestic animals, and zoning cases dealing with such issues. This appeared to be one of first impression in Pennsylvania, although I did find an appellate decision from Texas that held a horse can live anywhere it wants, although the same was not necessarily true regarding humans.

The zoning board started the hearing on time, and soon the overflow crowd jockeyed for the remaining standing room. Everyone was there: horse people, representatives from the SPCA, members of the neighborhood watch group, newspaper reporters, and the just plain curious.

"Are there any objectors to this application?" the chairperson asked.

"Yes." Some important looking guy stood up. He made a sophisticated movement of his manicured hand, as if he had just bid a few million dollars at auction for a French masterpiece.

"Hey! That's my neighbor, Snowman W. Doe," Mrs. Kleppelmyer exclaimed.

"Well," I hypothesized, "I'll bet a bucket of oats he's the guy who started this whole mess."

And he was. After we presented our well-reasoned case, Doe sauntered up to the microphone to give his side of the story.

"Look," he began, "I didn't build a $750,000 crib so I could live next door to a horse. If that's what I wanted, I would have bought a farm. And that's where *that nag* belongs."

A tear began to form in Mrs. Kleppelmyer's eye. I hate it when people cry at zoning hearings. Funerals, yes. Hearings, no. It breaks my concentration.

"It's a *miniature* horse," I blurted out.

"And so it only draws *miniature* flies? Is that your point, counsellor?" Snowman shouted.

And so the hearing went, back and forth. What about the horse manure? There wasn't any. It was wrapped up in the garbage. What about disease? The horse had all its shots. What about the smell? Well, I wanted to tell the board the horse would get used to Doe with time, but I decided to keep that remark to myself.

Then the hearing board members excused themselves to deliberate. The animated different camps surrounded my client and Doe, each expounding upon the merits of his or her respective position. Pickles was probably back at home, serenely unaware of the commotion she was causing. If Doe prevailed, the horse would be houseless, Mildred's kids would be petless, and Doe - he'd still be heartless.

- - - - - - - - - - - - - - - - - - -

There's something about people and animals that defies logic. I remember representing Burton Skagg, who was accused of murder, and rightfully so. He had intentionally committed arson, and in the process three innocent people died. He was found guilty, and so the next phase of the trial, the sentencing hearing, began. The jury had to decide on life in prison or death by lethal injection. I sensed that the 12 citizens were leaning in favor of my client. After all, there were some mitigating factors supporting a lenient sentence of life in prison. Then the district attorney pulled out his trump card: He confirmed that an Irish setter puppy had also perished in the blaze. Skagg was dead two weeks after his unsuccessful appeal was denied.

- - - - - - - - - - - - - - - - - - - -

Then the deliberation room door opened and the zoning board members shuffled out. Forty-five minutes! They had been talking a long time. It was hard to tell from their faces what secret they shared. Mildred held her breath. So did I.

Chapter 24
Confrontation At The O.K. Corral

CHAPTER 25

THE SKY IS FALLING...THE SKY IS FALLING

The First National Bank of Bethlehem was founded 1,902 years after the birth of Christ. To commemorate this milestone, the bank trustees carved the institution's date of incorporation into the marble facade above the towering columns supporting the depository's front entrance:

M C M I I

The trustees chose the recognized and established Latin numbering system, a mathematical language that, similar to the bank, had withstood the test of time. For as a priest once told me, Latin isn't dead, it's just sleeping. "M" has stood as the abbreviation for the number "1,000" for MM or perhaps MMM years. Perhaps it's the reason some candy manufacturers have chosen to place M&M on their product: They make thousands and thousands daily. It is the reason why McDonald's has a big M on each of its signs, why the word "millennium" starts with the letter M, and why millipedes have been known to leave behind thousands of footprints. M is imprinted on our one dollar bill as part of the date MDCCLXXVI, to reflect the annuit coeptis of our nations's novus ordo seclorum. The Bureau of Engraving wouldn't have it any other way.

- - - - - - - - - - - - - - - - - - - -

It was toward the end of the last century, about MCMLXXXX, when the first hint of impending doom began to surface. My father's generation had already survived Hitler, the atomic age, the cold war, and AIDS. How could there be anything left for me to confront? Then my computer repair guy mentioned a "minor" problem in passing, almost as an afterthought.

He had just finished reassembling the monitor on my secretary's desk. The week before the screen had "blinked" for a second or two, and in the process, lost more than 300 pages of recently typed material. For about half an hour, my secretary just sat there, her mouth open, staring at the blank screen. I gave her the rest of the day off. Such is progress.

"Larry," my computer guru, Ralph, remarked as he packed up his tool kit, "I don't think your system is Y2K compliant."

I hate it when things aren't compliant.

"What's Y2K?" I asked innocently. It would be the beginning of a long journey into night.

"It stands for the *Year 2000*, Ralph explained.

I have always disliked *abs*, which is my abbreviation for the word *abbreviation*. Abs perform a disservice upon those not privy to the meaning of the shortened term, thereby causing certain confusion. When I buy a pound of food, I don't want it measured in lbs. (By the way, this is an abbreviation for the Latin word *libra*, the ancient Roman pound that contained 5,053 grains.)

"Ralph," I politely corrected, "you mean Y2M."

"K."

"M," I insisted. "It's on the facade of the First National Bank which houses Ms of one dollar bills with Ms on them."

"K. It stands for *kilo*, which is the Greek prefix meaning *thousand*, introduced from the French in the nomenclature of the metric system."

"But you're mixing up the measurement of weight with the computation of time," I noted.

"They're interchangeable. Every year, I gain another lb.," Ralph sighed.

"Y2K makes no sense," I persisted. "People will laugh at you."

"Not at me, buddy," Ralph replied. "At any rate, you face non-compliance."

"But what does that *mean*?"

"On December 31, 1999, at the stroke of midnight, your computer will cease functioning."

"It will? Are you sure?"

His powers of prophecy astounded me.

"Yup. The calendar clock in your computer isn't programmed to turn to the year 2000. It stops on the last minute of 1999."

"But I just bought this computer from you two years ago. You didn't say anything about planned obsolescence back then."

"No one in the computer business gave it much thought. The next century seemed pretty far off. Now it's definitely a problem."

"Well, I'm no computer whiz, but can't I just type in 2000 when the new century rolls around?"

"Nice try. The computer will default back to the 20th century," Ralph noted flatly.

I stared at the blank screen that had just eaten 300 pages of labor-intensive typing, then I gazed at Ralph's blank face, as I thought about the blank check I would need to write out for a new computer. I wondered what Ralph would have done if Sears had sold him a water heater that planned to burst one minute prior to the turn of the century.

- - - - - - - - - - - - - - - - - - - -

The Supreme Court of Pennsylvania has ordered that every attorney practicing within the Commonwealth must attend 12 credit hours of seminars a year to keep current with changes in the law. The only members of the legal profession exempt from this requirement are the justices of the Supreme Court of Pennsylvania, since they are the reason changes in the law keep occurring.

It was January of MCMLXXXXIX. Only one year remained until the turn of the century, and the ensuing chaos that would result from massive computer meltdown. I began to scan the Bar Association list of dozens of seminars to see which topics caught my fancy. Ah, here was a one-credit class to be given in Harrisburg: *Tax Planning for the Distribution of Estate Residue to the Decedent's Post Mortum Legatees.*

Hmmmm. Gripping.

And then I saw it, half way down on the second page. A two-hour course to be presented in Mifflintown in March - more than eight months before life as we knew it was to end: *The Legal Effects of Y2K Non-compliance: Disaster on the Horizon.*

That was a seminar I didn't want to miss.

Signing up isn't always easy. I recall the last seminar I tried to attend, *Useful Techniques in Avoiding Bad Debts.* I called up the Pennsylvania Bar seminar reservation hot line in Harrisburg.

"Welcome to the Pennsylvania Bar Association," the recorded message began. "We are the lawyer's friend and your other partner in the practice of law. Please stay on the line for the next available representative."

I felt safe and secure. Here was an organization that loved me for who I am.

"Reservation Hot Line. How may I help you?"

"Hi. This is Larry Fox. May I sign up for a seminar?"

"Certainly, Mr. Fox. Are you an attorney and member of the Pennsylvania Bar Association?"

"Yes."

"Your Supreme Court I.D. number, please."

I gave it to her. I heard the computer beep as it digested the information.

"What seminar, please?"

"Useful Techniques In Avoiding Bad Debts. It's scheduled next week in Philadelphia."

"Very well, Mr. Fox. What credit card will you be using?"

"Credit card?"

"I'll need the sixteen-digit number and your expiration date."

She had caught me off guard since I wasn't planning to expire just yet. I hesitated.

"Can't I pay when I get there? I don't like giving credit card information over the phone."

"Mr. Fox, you know what they say ... Never take a check if a credit card is available."

Apparently she hadn't heard of the "Cash Consumer Protection Act," the act that prohibits discrimination against those who do not wish to pay by credit card. On the other hand, I was already learning an invaluable technique on how the Bar Association protected itself from a potential bad debt. I gave her my sixteen-digit credit card number.

I wasn't so hesitant signing up for the Y2K non-compliance seminar. I anticipated the credit card question, and I figured it didn't really matter. We'd all be dead by the time the bill arrived.

The massive course booklet, jammed in an oversized envelope, arrived three days later. I scanned the preface.

Your course planner, Alan Sapperhorn, Esquire, is a leading authority and expert on the Y2K dilemma facing both this state, and the world. He has authored several technical papers regarding the approaching calamity and its legal impact upon any survivors.

I looked into the mirror. I wasn't an expert on anything. How had Sapperhorn gained all this knowledge? Would he save himself, thereby becoming the father of the next human race?

I summoned the courage to turn the page and scan the table of contents. There was cause for pause:

Chapter 1. Nuclear power plants, trains, planes, and elevators. Why they will stop functioning.

Chapter 2. The Asian Rift. International non-compliance.

Chapter 3. Representing the non-compliant client. Unearthing records from hospitals, cemeteries, banks.

Chapter 4. Governmental disintegration: From the FAA to the Social Security Administration.

Chapter 5. Purchasing compliant computers: Breaking the upgrade news to the staff.

Chapter 6. What if you live? Problems facing survivors in the coming century.

Chapter 7. Non-compliancy lawsuits: Will you be the suer or suee?

Chapter 8. Hints on proper storage of food and water in your underground office bunker.

Chapter 9. The effect of non-compliance upon interrupted interplanetary space travel, and the resulting communication problems with alien beings.

How had the world permitted itself to fall into such a trap? Computers were espoused as our work-saving friends. Now they signaled our demise, similar to the seemingly harmless importation of killer bees. Worse yet, like a condemned prisoner, we all knew the exact minute when doom would fall upon us. Or did we? Would the west coast be doom-free three hours longer than the east coast? But why move to Los Angeles? You'd die in a week from the pollution.

March rolled around. Another day closer to the apocalypse. I grabbed the wheel of my obsolete Oldsmobile, and headed toward Mifflintown. I wanted all my seminar credits under my belt before the Bar Association computers crashed and automatically placed me on the *inactive suspended attorney* list. I knew if I ended up in that dreaded category, once the earth resumed spinning on its axis, it would be tough getting reinstated.

About 120 credit-seeking lawyers arrived at the Holiday Inn conference center located in the middle of town. Everyone was enjoying coffee and donuts, as if nothing was wrong. At the stroke of midnight on December 31, computers would no longer order the ingredients to make coffee or donuts, and the world as we know it was going to fade to black. Then what would all these light-hearted folks do? Sapperhorn was there too, jovial and smiling, like someone thrilled to chair an AIDS seminar.

"Please take your seats," he announced.

Everyone complied. Sapperhorn wasted no time. There was precious little left. During the first five introductory minutes he explained why the microscopic memory chip in non-compliant computers was incapable of operating in the 21st century.

"The result, of course, as reflected in Chapter One of my handout, will be that non-compliant trains, planes, subways, and nuclear power plants, just to mention a few systems we rely upon, will simply stop functioning. You don't want to be riding in an elevator at 11:59 p.m. on December 31st."

Elevator! The dangers in that little excursion seemed rather minor compared to a plane at 36 M feet. An old airman joke popped into my head: What's the difference between a single-engine and a twin-engine airplane? With a twin, if one engine quits, the other will take you to the scene of the accident.

"Now if planes start falling out of the sky and nuclear power plants melt down, there may be some lawsuits," Sapperhorn theorized.

It was becoming clear why this observant guy was an expert in his field.

"Chapter Two addresses the *Asian Problem*," Sapperhorn explained, the glow of his enthusiasm enveloping my fellow conference attendees. "As non-compliance from computers in Singapore and Hong Kong spreads across the Pacific, it will be only a matter of hours until our stock market is affected. About eight hours later, repercussions will hit the East Coast like a tsunami. Cows will go unmilked as automatic tit-sucking machines fail to activate. The Atlantic City gambling industry will shut down, resulting in New Jersey having no visible means of income other than permit fees for refuse disposal. Next door, the lights will go out in New York City, causing a miscalculation in birthrate projections. People will try to escape into Pennsylvania, but the tollgates won't work on the Delaware River Bridge."

I left the daylong seminar, shaken and despondent. Why had I worked so hard all these years, just to see my life disintegrate because of a defective computer chip? Sleep that evening was restless and intermittent. At 2:00 a.m. I dreamed there was a knock at my front door. I opened it.

"Special delivery," the snappy postal carrier announced.

"But it's two o'clock in the morning!" I protested as I rubbed my eyes.

"There's no time to waste, Bub. Things are coming to an end. The government sent this priority." He saluted, turned, and departed into the darkness.

I closed the door and stared at the letter. It was from the Social Security Administration. I had been paying into that unseen monolithic entity for more than three decades. Soon, I might actually get my due. I ripped open the communiqué.

Dear Taxpayer:

As you are aware, the government doesn't have enough money to purchase Y2K compliant computers. It was simply assumed from an actuarial standpoint that most of you would expire before a problem arose. Please be advised that as of January 1, 2000, your records will no longer exist. Should you have any questions, contact the voice mail system at your nearest Social Security Office before 12/31/99.

Sincerely,

The Social Security Administrator

Form Letter #837-a
Dictated - Not Read

In the morning, I awoke from a disquieting sleep. Jumping out of bed, I searched in vain for the damned letter. What would become of me? I'm just a lawyer, not a paralegal or receptionist. Pension? What pension?

And that wasn't the only nightmare that stinking seminar engendered. Two other recurring dreams began to terrorize me on a weekly basis, starting with the vision of the Pennsylvania Supreme Court Justice knocking at my law office door.

"Who is it?"

"Chief Justice Grimreaper."

"What do you want?"

"I was just in the neighborhood, so I thought I'd drop by to give you the news personally."

"What news?"

"Our computers show you're one credit shy. I'm afraid you'll have to turn out the lights, lock the door and come with me."

"That's impossible! I accumulated four extra credits this year."

"Maybe yes, maybe no. See, our computers are non-compliant so most of your records vanished."

I'd finally drift off to sleep, only to fall prey to another seminar-induced nightmare.

I see myself sitting in front of the TV. It's New Year's Eve, 1999, and the big, lighted ball is about to make its descent above Times Square in New York City. Thousands of people are dancing in the streets. Evidently, not one of them had attended the Y2K seminar in Mifflintown. It's true what they say: Ignorance is bliss. Seven - six - five - we're all going to die - four - three - two - one - Happy New Year! Then the TV set begins to flicker and my house lights go out.

All is eerily quiet, except for the overhead sputtering of a plane's dying engine.

Chapter 25
The Sky Is Falling...The Sky is Falling

CHAPTER 26

THE PLOT THICKENS

I've been practicing law for so long I can't remember when I wrote my first will and testament or for whom I wrote it. Over the past 30 years, I've written hundreds of them. The irony is that I probably won't even know when I've written my last will and testament. Like most of the other attorneys around here, they'll just find me slumped at my desk with my boots on, the dictating machine still whirring. It's a living, helping others prepare for death.

I walked into my conference room to find Herbert and Ethel Sopwith waiting. They had come to consult me about a will and testament, perhaps their first and last. Ethel had that despondent "look" about her - the one I had seen on a thousand faces in this very room. "If I sign a will, it will probably hasten my death. Maybe I should reschedule."

"How you folks doin' today?" I quipped just the way my proctologist has always chosen to greet me, my bare ass pointed skyward where Nurse Ratchet positioned it 30 minutes earlier. I never answer, since my face is buried in the examination table wax paper.

Ethel couldn't answer either. She was too emotionally distraught. That's why I keep a box of tissues nearby. Stoic Herbert was in a league of his own. He knew each beat of his heart brought him one step closer to the abyss. He didn't want to be caught unprepared, slumped over a desk.

"Get a grip," he snarled as he rolled his eyes at his wife of 42 years.

This delicate moment in Ethel's life called for sympathy - nothing less.

"She's always complaining about something," Herbert explained, as he rubbed his forehead impatiently.

I had never met this couple before. I knew nothing about them. But I wondered how Ethel had put up with this insensitivity for all these years. I began to ask my standard litany of questions.

Yes, they were husband and wife. Yes, they were residents of Pennsylvania. No, they had never drafted a will before.

"Do you have any children?" I inquired.

Ethel stopped wiping her eyes long enough to respond.

"Just Pussy."

A daughter? I began to write.

"That's our cat," she corrected as she pointed to my notes.

I was relieved. Imagine the horrendous teasing....

Ethel's eyes grew wide.

"Oh my God!" she blurted out.

"What now?" Herbert mumbled.

"Pussy!" Her serious brown eyes turned to me. "What would happen to her if Herbert and I died simultaneously? Can we make arrangements for Pussy in the will?"

"Are you out of your mind?" Herbert gasped.

Herbert probably wasn't aware, but I get this question *all* the time.

"Certainly," I consoled her. "You can nominate a guardian with whom Pussy might reside, and a trustee who would administer an account to assure that Pussy's future financial needs are met."

"You mean I could set aside money to make sure she's properly fed and cared for?"

"Oh for God sakes!" Herbert interjected.

Ethel was on a roll. "Would you be the trustee? I trust you," she added quickly.

"I'm honored by your request, Mrs. Sopwith," I assured her, "but I'm over 55. Pussy might very well outlive us both. Isn't there someone younger you might nominate?"

Ethel took a moment to think. I moved on to the next issue.

"Do you own any real estate?"

"Our home," said Herbert.

"And our burial plot," Ethel reminded him gently. She turned to me. "It's in consecrated ground at Holy Savior Cemetery on Center Street. We bought it when we got married, so we'd always be together."

"It was on special," Herbert clarified. "I got a good price."

"The plots?" I inquired.

"There's just one plot," Ethel corrected me.

"Like a bunk bed," Herbert explained. "One body gets buried on top of the other. A two-fer!" he boasted.

Ethel squirmed in her seat. During the last 30 years of will drafting, I had been asked a lot of strange questions. One lady wanted to be buried in her Jaguar convertible to assure a stylish ride heavenward. One client left instructions to be laid to rest in his duck-hunting thermal underwear and woolen socks in case he got cold. The customer is always right. I put the requests in their wills.

"Is there something else, Mrs. Sopwith?"

"As a matter of fact..."

Herbert nearly jumped out of his chair.

"Now what? We're paying this guy by the hour."

Ethel was on a mission. She could not be distracted.

"If I die first, can I be buried a second time - you know - dug up again?"

The convertible Jaguar question was a snap compared to this. A temporary resurrection. Hmmmm. Ethel noted my hesitation.

"See, the plot requires that somebody be on the bottom. So, if I die first, that'll be me. I want the top. So if I die before Herbert, I'd like to be removed until Herbert is inserted. O.K.?"

Herbert went ashen. Apparently, this minor issue had never been discussed. He gazed at her as if she were committable.

"What could it possibly matter who's on top and who's...I mean you're dead! Get it?" he snapped. "The important thing is that we got a hell of a deal on this hole - in consecrated God damned ground no less. What could it possibly matter who goes in first?"

"It matters to me."

"Why? Damn it. Why?"

"Because for this whole hell-on-earth marriage, you've been on the top. I've been on the bottom. I'm not spending eternity the same way."

Chapter 26
The Plot Thickens

CHAPTER 27

SHORTY'S LAST FLIGHT

Nowadays, a college student off for the summer looking for work usually settles for a minimum wage job nobody else wants. The remuneration is a joke - not even enough to pay for use of the family car. Back when I was an undergraduate, things were a little different. I worked four summers for Bethlehem Steel Corporation, as did hundreds of other youngsters who temporarily joined a local work force of 12,000, manufacturing hot steel on three shifts around the clock. I paid union dues, and received union wages. I was, when not attending school, a steelworker, like my father and grandfather before me.

One middle shift I reported to No. 8 machine shop as part of an itinerant labor gang. Soon I found myself ankle deep in used machine oil, standing in an eight-foot pit under an enormous rotating lathe spewing forth red-hot ringlets of smoking steel. My job was to shovel this unending shower of discarded by-product into a cavernous storage container that was periodically lifted by crane above floor elevation for transition to a waiting scrap train.

Clothed in my hard-hat, heavy-duty gloves, eye protectors, respirator, metatarsal shoes, and fire-resistant suit, I became a gladiator poised for battle. Periodically, some safety inspector would peer down at me, or a foreman would pass by at the edge of the pit and jot down on his ever-present clipboard that I appeared to be alive. Then he'd walk out of view to the next darkened hole, where he'd check on some other oil-soaked kid under a neighboring lathe.

The noise and confusion never stopped. Cranes dropped chains and hooks from the rafters, lathes the size of mobile homes rotated effortlessly, hot chips flew onto my shoulders, train whistles blew, and skilled machinists created the instruments of war from 10-ton blocks of gleaming alloy steel.   Above me, they ground the base for a future submarine's nuclear generator. Tolerances of accuracy were measured in hundredths of a centimeter - all this before the age of computers.

Two hours had passed and still the glowing chips continued to cascade around me. I dumped another shovel load into the bottomless waste receptacle. And that's when I first noticed them - perhaps as many as 16 hard hats and covered faces staring down at me as they surrounded my pit on all four sides. What had I done - or failed to do - to draw so much attention?

Although I stared upward through grimy safety glasses, it was nonetheless clear that these folks were not hourly wage-earning grunts. They were aliens from a world of hand-tailored suits and crisp white shirts. A world of high society and golf outings. These folks had never stood in an oil pit while dodging discarded steel chips. After a few minutes, the entourage moved on without so much as a parting wave.   By mid-afternoon they would probably conduct an interview with the New York Times.

During the 7:00 p.m. lunch break, I would learn that I had been part of a tour by none other than the President of Bethlehem Steel Corporation, accompanied by the Secretary of the United States Navy, and a few of their close friends.

The President of Bethlehem Steel!   The man in charge of more than 50,000 employees world-wide, and this day he had chosen to look at me. I was aware this Fortune 500 company had a president, but I never dreamed I'd ever actually *see* him. After all, rumor had it he lived in the off-limits gated community behind the restricted country club, and only emerged from his chauffeur-driven car on rare occasions.

The President of Bethlehem Steel! He could, by just snapping his fingers, choose which one of three corporate jets would instantaneously whisk him around the world to check on corporate holdings. His summer home in the tropics was more palatial than the White House, and why not? He was paid seven times as much as the President of the United States. I had never dreamed that I would come so close to meeting such a dignitary.

- - - - - - - - - - - - - - - - - - - -

Frank "Shorty" Vanchick stopped by my hangar to say hello. He stood just 5' 4" tall, but walked as a giant among the fraternity of local aviators. His entire life had been dedicated to the art of flight. Had he been born before the invention of the airplane, his life would have been meaningless. Everything he thought about, every effort he expended, pursued the singular goal of escaping the earth's gravitational constraints.

There was no conventional aircraft he had not flown, neither in defense of his country, as an instructor, nor as a commercial pilot. There was no exotic location he could not describe from personal experience. He had been pilot in command of props, helicopters, jets, and anything else that left the land or water. He held every rating a pilot could achieve. His enthusiasm when discussing the science of flight was infectious.

Frank was chief pilot for Bethlehem Steel Corporation. After his discharge from the military, he joined the industrial giant, and quickly rose through the ranks. It was he and his staff of five co-pilots who transported "The Steel's" corporate executives around the world.

Frank and I had become close friends. His small private plane and mine were hangared next to each other at the local airport. On weekends we'd swap lies about flying as we cleaned and maintained our aircraft.

"I turn 65 in three more weeks," he lamented as he leaned against the fuselage of my plane.

"I know," I said. "Mandatory retirement."

"It isn't fair, it just isn't fair. I'm a better pilot now than I was 50 years ago," Frank explained.

The hated moment of reckoning was fast approaching. In just a few days Frank would have to retire

176

as Bethlehem's chief pilot. The thought of being pushed out to pasture made him cringe.

"Twenty-five years of trouble-free flight, and they throw me away like yesterday's newspaper," he said.

"I wish there was something I could do," I offered my hurt friend.

"Actually, there is," he confided.

"Oh?"

"Yes. My last flight is in three weeks. I'll ferry the President to London for the annual European Iron and Steel conference. That's where you come in."

"Me?" I laughed.

"What's so funny?"

"Nothing. It's just that 30 years ago, I looked up from a steel mill oil pit and saw his predecessor's predecessor."

"Not to worry. They're both dead. Now here's the plan. You have a security pass to get inside the airport gate. Right?"

"Right..." I heard myself say.

"O. K. Here goes ... before my last flight, you need to...

- - - - - - - - - - - - - - - - - - -

I don't actually recall agreeing to join this conspiracy, but three weeks later, I was, without question, an accomplice.

The Bethlehem Steel hangar stood as the largest structure on the field. It was bigger than the passenger terminal building. It housed three gleaming corporate jets, and all of the personnel and equipment required to maintain them. It was a city within a city, with its own galley and berthing area for pilots and support crew. There was a weather briefing room, fire and emergency rescue center, and a private security office.

The big day had finally arrived. Shorty drove me to the corporate hangar. A private police force guarded the spotless jets as they reposed in the hushed atmosphere of the massive building. Shorty waved politely to one of the cops as he ushered me into his private office. The gold lettering on his door read Chief Pilot. He quickly shut the door behind us and locked it.

"No time to spare," he instructed. "Estimated time of departure is 0945."

He raced to his closet. Inside was stored a large collection of his pressed pilot uniforms. He rummaged behind them and produced a crisp white ambulance driver's uniform, complete with shoes and hat.

"Here, put these on," he commanded.

Next came a folding wheelchair - and a stuffed duffel bag.

"You have no idea how difficult it was getting this past security," he confided.

I scrambled into my disguise, emerging as a certified "Medic" - or so it said on the back of my uniform.

Shorty dressed himself in his handsome pilot suit and matching slacks with four gold captain stripes circling the cuffs above his wrists. Then he sat down in the wheelchair and opened the duffel bag.

"Now help me with the finishing touches," he requested.

He pulled out a fake plaster arm cast he had cut in two halves. He placed them around his right arm and taped them shut. "O. K. Can you help me fit this bandage splint around my arm and neck?"

Next came a similar cast for his left leg, encapsulating his limb from ankle to hip.

"How do I look?" he inquired.

"Like you got hit by a bus," I assured him.

"Good," he confirmed. "Now for the piece de resistance."

He reached into the bag with his good hand and brought forth one more fake bandage.

"Put this on my forehead," he beamed.

Suddenly, the chief pilot appeared to have lost sight in his right eye.

"Now, I think we're ready," he confirmed. He picked up a telephone on his desk and dialed security.

"Has the co-pilot completed the pre-flight? ... Good ... Are all passengers on board? ... Good."

"Let's go," he ordered in my direction as he limped over to the wheelchair and sat down, his broken leg now stretched out in front of him.

I unlocked the office door, and wheeled my patient down the hallway and into the immense hangar. A twin-engine jet awaited us, its cargo of corporate executives being served its first round of cocktails. The whine of the motors had begun to escalate as the co-pilot, unaware of what was about to happen, began his routine warm-up procedures.

I followed Shorty's instructions to the letter. There was no backing out now. I pushed the wheelchair and its injured occupant to the folding gangplank that stretched from the polished hangar floor eight steps up to the captain's flight deck. Shorty struggled to extricate himself from the wheelchair. Then he began the arduous journey up the stairs by hopping backwards, using his one functioning leg, as his injured leg stuck straight out in its cast.

The President of Bethlehem Steel always sat in the first passenger seat. Corporate pecking order so directed. As he sipped his drink, he happened to glance out his porthole. What he saw caught his attention, since he was safety conscious and about to embark on a 7-hour non-stop flight over the icy Atlantic. I saw him both spill his drink and hit his head as he shot out of his seat. In an instant, he stood looming at the top of the stairs, similar to his predecessors long passed, who had once stood towering above me in the oil pits.

"What the hell is going on here?" R. Jenkins Taylor barked as he gawked at Shorty, who was still gingerly inching himself up the gangplank. Shorty, who was proceeding with his back to the jet, bent his head upward and backward.

"Oh...Hi, Mr. Taylor. It should be a relatively uneventful flight."

"My God! What happened to you, Vanchick?"

"Nothing earth-shattering. Just me and a bus maneuvering for the same territory. They say the pins in the leg will keep my foot from turning sideways during the flight. It's not a serious compound fracture."

"Your goddamned eye! Your goddamned arm!"

"Not to worry, Sir. That's what co-pilots are for. My right arm is hardly scratched, and most of the important instruments are on that side," Shorty suggested as he continued to inch skyward. "The doctor gave me pills in case I become faint again. I'll have the steward put a glass of water next to my headset."

Security began to appear at the foot of the jet. The other passengers began moving to the gangplank door. They, too, seemed to be interested in Shorty's questionable state of health. This was the perfect time for me and my wheelchair to head back to the hangar. One thing was for sure. Shorty's last flight would, indeed, be memorable.

Chapter 27
Shorty's Last Flight

181

CHAPTER 28

GRANDPA'S GLASSES

Some of my fondest memories as a preschooler include those of my paternal grandparents. Grandpa and Grandma Fox were in their 60s and lived in retirement across the street from our home. I was welcomed into their snug Cape Cod without reservation. I felt loved and wanted, day or night, even though I often arrived at their door unannounced and most often looking for cake or cookies.

"Larry!" Grandma Fox would exclaim with delight as she opened the front door. "Grandpa was just wondering when you might be stopping by."

Despite her age, Grandma's voice had the sing-song clarity of an opera star - at least to me.

Grandpa and Grandma sought unintentionally to spoil me, and true to form, were the dead opposite of my folks. They accepted me unconditionally, they never criticized, and for reasons not understood by any 5-year-old, they sought to honor my every whim.

"Grandpa is waiting for you."

"O.K." I walked into the living room. There he was, as usual, seated in his overstuffed chair at the big mahogany table. My special chair with the board across the arm rests waited for me. By sitting on the board, we could talk man-to-man and eye-to-eye.

"Want to play cards?" he inquired.

"Uh huh," I confirmed. Grandpa always knew exactly what I wanted.

"How about Go Fish?"

Go Fish was my very favorite card game. It was also the only card game I knew. Grandpa had taught me to play three months earlier on my 5th birthday. The rules were complex. First, I had to shuffle the deck without dropping too many cards. Then Grandpa "cut" the deck.

"Why do you do that?" I asked.

"So no one deals off the bottom. That would be cheating."

"What's that?"

"What?"

"Dealing off the bottom?"

"Ask me when you turn six."

I couldn't wait to turn six. Grandpa agreed to answer dozens of pressing questions when I made it to first grade.

Next I had to deal one card to Grandpa and then one card to me, and then continue until we each had eight cards. Grandpa had also taught me how to count to eight, plus nine and ten and all the way up to 20.

I placed the remaining cards face down on the table, and studied the cards in my hand, arranging them so I could see each one. It wasn't easy to do this without dropping the slippery rectangles, so I'd hold four cards in each hand. Grandpa held all his cards in one hand. The other reached into his ever-present cigar box. There he produced a hand-rolled masterpiece with its own individual gold ring with raised insignia.

"You want the ring?"

"Of course, Grandpa." He handed me the paper ring. This ceremony required that I lay down all my cards, and place the ring on my middle finger. Having collected my cards once again, we were almost ready to play.

"Want to blow out the match?"

"Uh huh." I loved blowing out the match. It was almost as much fun as blowing out the candles on a birthday cake.

"Do you have any sixes?" I began.

Grandpa blew a smoke ring as he reviewed his cards. What an incredible talent! He studied my face as I watched the smoke ring travel heavenward, its swirling concentric figure remaining intact. It was time for the day's first man-to-man conversation.

"There's nothing better than a good Cuban cigar, Larry."

"Uh huh. What's a Cuban, Grandpa?"

"Cuba is an island where they make cigars."

"Who does?"

"The Cubans - the people who live there make the cigars."

"Oh."

"We've tried to make them here in America, but they're just not as good. If anything ever happens to Cuba, the world as we know it will come to an end."

"Can I smoke a cigar?"

"When you turn 21."

"When is that?"

"Let's see...that'd be 1969. So...in 16 more years."

"Will anything happen to Cuba before 1969?"

"No, the cigars are too important. There will always be a Cuba and there will always be Cuban cigars. In 1969 I'll be 81. You can light up your first cigar, give me the gold ring, and I'll blow out your match."

"O.K. Do you have any sixes?"

Grandpa again reviewed his cards. "No. Go fish."

I picked up one of the face down cards lying between us. It wasn't a six. I needed to collect three of a kind, so I might display them on the table face up. Whoever disposed of all of their cards by compiling three of a kind, won the game. Now it was Grandpa's turn.

"Do you have any...(the suspense was almost too much)...any queens?"

That was the card with the strange but colorful woman on it. Rats! I had one. That meant I had to give her majesty to Grandpa, and he'd have another turn.

"Do you have any...sevens?"

Whew! That was a close one. (I had an eight.) Grandpa was the best Go Fish player I had ever met.

In the space of just 10 minutes, Grandpa was only a guess or two from victory. And then it happened - the same miracle as the week before, and the week before that. Grandpa pushed his bifocal glasses slightly up the bridge of his nose, while simultaneously holding his cards an inch closer to his face. I could, once again, clearly see reflected in his bifocals each card in his hand.

"Do you have any fours?" I asked, already knowing the answer.

"As a matter of fact, I do," Grandpa confessed.

This correct guess empowered me to remain on the offensive.

"Do you have any tens?" Grandpa handed over the card as his glasses continued to betray him. My next five guesses were also correct, and I easily snatched victory from the jaws of defeat.

"You beat me again," he exclaimed in amazement. "You're sure good at this game." I shook my head up and down.

"Lunch anyone?" Grandma asked. She appeared at just the right moment, carrying sandwiches with the crust removed. Not even my mother understood the importance of removing the crust. Our hostess gave me a glass of milk and dutifully placed a glass of purple stuff in front of Grandpa. Then she vanished, knowing that there are times when men must be alone.

"What's *that*?" I questioned.

"Prune juice," Grandpa responded.

"Can I taste?"

"No, it's like cigars. You have to be a certain age. When you turn six I'll explain why you'll need it when you turn 64."

"Grandpa..."

"What?"

"I got to tell you something."

My elder could sense that I had grown serious. He put down his sandwich. It was time for another man-to-man talk.

"What's on your mind?"

"I didn't win the card game today, or last week."

"Yes you did. You guessed all the cards in my hand."

I started to squirm on the board spanning the armrests. "No, I didn't. I could see your cards in your glasses." I had just engaged in my first heartfelt confession at the ripe old age of five. Grandpa tried to look surprised.

"Is that so?"

"Yes."

"Why are you telling me this, Larry?"

"So you will hold your cards away from your glasses. I want to win fair and square."

"Larry..."

"What?"

"Do you know I've always loved you?"

"Yes."

"Now, I respect you."

Attorney Harvey Crumshackel had been actively engaged in the practice of law for more than half a century. He was a well-respected member of our bar who had earned his reputation as a tough, but fair representative of his clients. Now he faced the same milestone as other sole practitioners at the end of a long career: How do I hand over my practice? Who will take all my files? What number should my clients call if they need a file or have a question?

Harvey spotted me at the quarterly bar association dinner and asked to join me as the salads were being served.

"I'd be honored, Mr. Crumshackel," I assured the elder statesman as he propped his cane against the table, and gently inched into his chair. His body was beginning to fail, but not his mind.

"Please, just call me Harvey," he requested.

"Very well, Harvey. How have you been?"

"Not bad. Not bad at all. Is that butter?"

I passed the butter.

"Larry..."

"Yes?"

"My wife and I want to retire soon. I've been thinking about my practice. There are quite a few clients."

"I can only imagine."

"Well, I'm looking for someone, someone respectable, whose philosophy of the law matches mine. I need a lawyer who conducts himself and caters to the needs of my clients the way I always have. The search is more difficult than I had imagined."

"No doubt."

"But...your firm. You folks seem fair and ethical."

"Thank you for saying so."

"Would you work on a case or two, Larry, just to see if our methodology is in sync? No long-term commitments - just a chance to see how things develop."

"I appreciate the thought, Harvey. Let me share your idea with my partners." We shook hands.

And so it was that an informal relationship began with Harvey and my firm. None of us felt compelled to rush into a committed "marriage," but once in a while, Crumshackel would check in - always pleasant, professional, and to the point.

"Larry..."

"Good morning, Harvey."

"Good morning. How's life treating you?"

He went on to explain that his office represented a group of about 70 merchants leasing stores at the Easterbrook Shopping Mall. The merchant's association had been Harvey's client for years. It was time to renegotiate one of the leases, and Harvey wanted me on board. I'd get to meet one of the tenants and see how, as Harvey put it "the mall owners continuously try to beat up retailers for more rent." Harvey said he had a system he used to keep the rents low.

Two days later I met Harvey and our client, James Bennett, at the mall administrative offices. What a dump. When was the last time they had painted the place? When was the last time the cleaning service had stopped by?

The unframed reprint of some waterfowl soaring above a forgotten vase of artificial flowers did little to enhance the waiting area. My thoughts were interrupted by the receptionist who was chewing gum in such a manner that each time her bovine jaws made a movement, there emerged a popping sound. She spoke in a monotone as she communicated in one unending sentence. Her phone rang.

"Hel-lo-this-is-Coyle-may-I-help-you?"

She wore no make-up, no jewelry, and her pink sneakers did little to compliment her blue jogging suit. She did not smile or breath as she soaked in all the news in the *Soap Opera Gazette*. Once in a while she would clear her throat as she temporarily removed her gum to munch on twinkies.

Harvey, Bennett and I selected the worn yellow couch with the fewest coffee stains. We stared across the room at an unframed print of four cigar-smoking dogs playing poker. I thought about rescheduling the meeting at a more hospitable location, like the city dump, but Coyle had just received word that the assistant mall manager would soon grace us with his presence.

"Mr.-Samuels-will-see-youse-now," she advised, as she fingered the strand of love beads that encircled her pudgy neck. Perhaps she had been instrumental in designing her work area, an area that looked nothing like a traditional office.

We entered the windowless office of Bert Samuels, assistant mall administrator. He possessed that indescribable air about him that only affected my senses when I stood in the company of a time share realtor. But it was his personal touch at interior decorating that gave me a hint at what he found to be significant in life. On his desk, actually in the middle of his desk, sat an oversized lamp, the base of which was composed of an official National Football League-sanctioned reproduction of an Eagles football team helmet. The light was activated by pulling on shoestrings used to lace football shoes. On the rear wall was displayed an Eagles jersey. A team photo hung nearby, as did a large gold embossed schedule of last year's home games. He saw my mouth hanging open.

"So you're an Eagles fan, too," he offered in my direction. "You ought to see what I got at home...probably $500 just in official tailgate beer mugs."

Harvey made the introductions.

"This is James Bennett, our client. He operates the jewelry boutique on the lower level of the mall. And this is my co-counsel, Lawrence Fox."

"Nice to meet you gents. Why don't we go over to my conference table."

Samuels tucked his shirt in his pants and waddled over to a three-foot by four-foot portable card table accentuated with four folding chairs, each sporting the Eagles logo. An official Eagles ceiling fan light twirled above us. Someone had scraped most of the chewing gum off my seat, so I sat down.

"Now let's see," Samuels began as he flipped through a thick document, "Mr. Bennett's lease comes up for renewal in six months."

"Correct," Harvey confirmed.

"Well, as you guys are aware, the cost of running this here mall just keeps going up, so rent has to follow," he chuckled.

"Let me come to the point," Crumshackel interjected. "My client, Mr. Bennett, is barely making a profit after working mall hours, seven days a week for the last two and one-half years. He presently pays $11.00 a square foot. He can see his way to paying $11.25, but that's his limit."

Samuels, who sat across the table from Crumshackel, shook his head in sympathy, similar to an undertaker attempting to console a bereaved family.

"Are you kidding? All the merchants downstairs will be paying $17.50 by year's end. The offer is $17.25. Not a penny less."

Harvey wasn't convinced. "You've got three vacancies you can't fill now, and there are five malls within a 10-mile radius that will close a deal with us at $12.25."

"But those malls don't have the same customer base," Samuels countered.

For the next 15 minutes, the two negotiators debated the merits and disadvantages of life at the mall. Bennett and I remained silent spectators.

"Give me a minute," Harvey responded. "I've got to talk with my client."

We walked to the corner of the room, and huddled together as Harvey wrote a figure on his pad of paper. Bennett nodded up and down. We returned to the card table.

"This is my final offer," Harvey announced. "Take it or Mr. Bennett starts packing and you can have another vacancy."

Harvey dramatically raised his pad of paper to within a few inches of his bifocals, studied the figure one last time and proclaimed: "$11.50."

Samuels concentrated upon the poker face seated across from him, then responded. "$11.75, or it's no deal, Crumshackel."

Crumshackel looked at Bennett as Bennett looked at Crumshackel.

"Deal," Harvey confirmed. "But you sure drive a hard bargain."

Everyone stood up and shook hands.

"I'll send you the paperwork in the morning," Samuels assured us as we passed by the receptionist who didn't bother to look up. She was struggling with a soap opera jigsaw puzzle. Out in the hallway, Mr. Bennett thanked Harvey for a job well done, and then left in the direction of his store.

"Would Bennett actually have moved if that last offer had been refused?" I questioned.

"Probably not," Harvey responded. "Last week he authorized me to go up to $15.00."

"I'm impressed by your powers of persuasion."

"Don't be. That bottom-feeder Samuels gets all the credit. Apparently he can read figures backwards."

"I don't quite understand."

"I wrote '$11.75 FINAL OFFER' on my legal pad, just before I offered $11.50. Then I held the notepad at an angle so Samuels would see the higher figure reflected in my glasses. He probably deals off the bottom of the deck when he plays cards."

Chapter 28
Grandpa's Glasses

CHAPTER 29

SPRINKLES II

I served a hitch as an enlisted man in the United States Coast Guard Reserve. It was a good experience. We never killed anyone, and once in a while we'd save a life.

During the 200th birthday celebration of the Statue of Liberty, I received orders to report to New York Harbor for port security patrol. I joined a crew on a 44 foot 1600 horsepower surfboat. We, and scores of other "Coasties" were tasked with the responsibility of maintaining order among the hundreds of visiting watercraft and assuring that no terrorist activity took place.

To accomplish these goals, Coast Guard personnel were authorized to flag down any vessel at any time, with or without reason or probable cause. My shipmates and I carried out our orders. Our uninvited boardings were often rather dramatic. Three of us, all wearing 45 caliber side arms accompanied by a shotgun and M16 rifle, would scamper onto the deck of the detained vessel, and conduct a safety check. Depending upon the disposition of her crew and condition of the boarded ship, such inspections could continue for half an hour. Sometimes tempers flared and situations became confrontational.

The day of the big celebration, President Reagan and his entourage flew into the Coast Guard base of operations at Governors Island, the outcropping situated next to the Statue of Liberty. Dignitaries and celebrities from around the world joined him as invited yacht after yacht moored at our docks. My surfboat was assigned to patrol the security zone north of the Verrazano Narrows Bridge that connects Staten Island with Brooklyn. We headed out in moderate seas, with clear visibility. There were so many vessels gathered in New York's Upper Bay that it would have been possible to walk from Manhattan to New Jersey by stepping on the bows of neighboring ships.

There were more than 40 "tall ships" from around the world, each displaying its full sailing rigging. There were luxury liners loaded with gawking tourists. But it was the floating private palaces that were to be the focus of our attention this morning. Many of these yachts were designed and equipped to circumnavigate the globe.

Our boatswain's mate spotted the first victim of the day, a 120-foot sleek three-deck craft trolling in the narrows of the Upper Bay. Gold lettering on its stern identified the yacht as *Sprinkles II*. The boatswain's mate pulled out a bullhorn to announce our intentions.

"Ahoy there Sprinkles II. Stand fast for a security boarding by the United States Coast Guard."

We had been trained for just about any contingency: undocumented aliens, illegal drugs, contraband, safety violations, even terrorists. We completed a final check of our weapons, and tied up alongside our towering quarry. The boatswain's mate, accompanied by a second-class port security petty officer, and I climbed up the exterior stair railing of the swaying yacht, and ascended onto the main deck.

Sprinkles II was a beauty. She boasted air conditioned individual berthing areas for 12, a stocked galley for the on-board private chef, hot showers, a crew of six, and mahogany paneled living quarters with every conceivable amenity. The control room was the kind featured in *Sailing Monthly*. It had the most modern panel of seagoing navigational aids imaginable, including satellite weather computer, wireless Internet modem, fax machine, autopilot, and radar. Twin diesel engines capable of illuminating a hospital hummed below decks.

In the midst of all this opulence sat the owner, perhaps 70 years of age, along with his wife (about 34), and a dozen of his closest nautical buddies. He was dressed in Bermuda shorts, a tee shirt, and torn sneakers. He probably didn't know how to steer the boat, much less which end pointed forward. His biggest concern appeared to be his morning bowel of oatmeal.

"Do we have any bananas?" he inquired of the waiter.

After about 15 minutes of investigation, we determined that these were not terrorists, despite the crew's foreign accents, and that there were no safety violations. It was time to abandon ship and end our unwanted imposition on this captain's private domain. But curiosity had taken possession of me. Who was this guy? And what was with the name *Sprinkles II*?

"Captain, with your permission, we'll be departing your vessel," I advised.

"Huh? You still here? O. K. That will be fine. Thank you."

"Captain..." I added.

"Now what?" he replied.

"May I ask a question?"

My host placed the spoon in his cereal bowl and motioned for me to take a seat. I made $35 a day as a third class enlisted man in the Coast Guard. I was now floating on a yacht that cost more to maintain than the State of Rhode Island, a yacht on which the pot scrubber made $35 an hour. I needed to know. Was I addressing the president of Ford Motor Company on his day off?

"Captain, did you name this vessel?"

"Yup."

"Is there any significance to the name?"

"You like ice cream?" my host interrupted.

"Yes Sir."

"Want some?"

"Now? It's 8 in the morning!"

"Never too early, and never too late for ice cream, son." The old man looked around. "Where the hell's the steward?"

A waiter appeared out of nowhere, dressed in white shoes, white pants, and a blue blazer. The old man handed him the cereal bowl.

"Damned doctors. What do they know? Take this mush and get us some real food." He turned to me. "You like tutti-frutti?"

"Excuse me," I said.

"Don't tell me you're a chocolate or vanilla sort of a guy. You can tell an awful lot about people by the flavor ice cream they eat."

"Sure. I like tutti-frutti."

"Thought so. You're O.K., Admiral."

He turned to the steward. "Two tutti-frutties...Wait a minute! You want sprinkles?" he inquired.

"Sprinkles?"

"SPRINKLES, son. I own all the Uncle Sprinkles Ice Cream franchises between here and Key West. Every time some kid comes in for a treat, we ask if he wants sprinkles. That costs an extra quarter. The quarter goes in a jar. When I have enough quarters I buy a yacht. I'm saving up for my third one now."

Chapter 29
Sprinkles II

CHAPTER 30

THE ROLLBACK

"I have a problem. You've got to help me!"

It was Cranston Trembly again. He was a long-time client and a good friend. He owned and operated the used car lot at the end of town. Believe it or not, he managed to earn a reputation for honest and ethical dealing. "Trembly Pre-Owned Cars" stickers adorned the back bumpers of vehicles from Klecknersville to Palmerton. This wasn't a fluke. Cranston, and his father before him, ran their above-board business in our small town for close to 50 years. He treated his customers, most of whom ultimately purchased second, third, and fourth cars, fairly and with respect.

But now, there was fear in his voice.

"What's wrong, Cranston?"

"I just received a certified letter from the Pennsylvania Attorney General - Office of Consumer Protection. It doesn't sound like an invitation to afternoon tea. Can I bring this over?"

He made it to the office in less than 10 minutes.

"What is this?" he asked. I read the letter, addressed to *Trembly Used Cars*.

Gentlemen:

A complaint has been filed with this office by Veronica Fromp alleging that you sold her a motor vehicle whose odometer mileage reading was, without her knowledge, intentionally altered. The automobile, a 1999 Buick Skylark, vehicle identification A734491218BJD, was purchased at your franchise by the complainant on or about June 24, 2003, and at time of purchase the odometer reading was displayed and advertised as 23,040 miles. A subsequent investigation has revealed that the digit to the left of the above display was rolled back, and that the actual vehicular mileage was, at time of sale, 123,040.

If you dispute the above allegation, contact this office within 10 days of receipt of this letter. Refer to Complaint No. A37-412.

Very truly yours,

J.T. Rollins
Assistant Attorney General
Division of Motor Vehicle Fraud

I looked up from my reading to find Cranston staring at me.

"Cranston, c'mon. You've never engaged in fraudulent conduct. You're as honest as the day is long. You're not going to jail. Now, tell me what you know." I saw him exhale.

"See, it's like this. Every Thursday my driver Buddy and I go to Cromwell's Auto Auction to pick up a car or two."

"The one in Jersey?"

"Yeah...So I see this 1999 Buick and she's a cream puff. There's not a mark on her and low mileage, too. Only 24,000 miles. They were about to put it on the block just as I got there. I had maybe two minutes to make up my mind. No sooner had I looked under the hood with seven or eight other bidders, than the auctioneer starts the sale. Somebody yells $2,800, somebody else $2,900. I knew I'd be able to resell that puppy for $4,950, so I joined the bidding. I finally got her for $3,400. So Buddy drives the Buick back and I followed in our pick-up. I didn't have the car on the lot two days, before this Fromp lady shows up all excited. *I just gotta have this car. I just gotta,* she says. So I sold it to her for $4,950. She got a deal, 'cause the next day some guy stops in and offers me more. 'Nope,' I says, 'I promised it already and my word is my bond.' Now I wish I had sold it to him."

"Why?"

199

"A week goes by and Fromp is back. Says she was cheated.

"Cheated says I. What's wrong?

"She says the mileage was rolled back. The Buick actually has 124,000 on it, not 24,000.

"How does she know, I ask.

"She says she did a title search and learned some guy named Sassaman sold the car to the auction company. Some guy named Thurgood previously sold the car to Sassaman. When Thurgood registered the car in Jersey last year, he reported the odometer reading as 120,000 miles. Six months later when Sassaman took title, Sassaman reported only 20,000. When the Buick sold at auction, it showed 24,000 miles."

"So Sassaman performed the illegal 100,000 mile roll-back?" I hypothesized.

"I guess, but how do you prove it?" Cranston responded.

"Was there any way you could have known before buying the car that a roll-back of the mileage had occurred?"

"Two ways. If I had had more than a couple minutes before the auction, I could have pulled out my lap top computer, and done a title check myself. Sometimes you get a response the same day. And there's another little test every car dealer knows."

"What's that?"

"Look at the wear on the rubber gas accelerator pedal. It's a sure giveaway."

"Was it worn?"

"Nope. Looked brand new. That Sassaman guy must have changed it. Pretty smooth operator. Well, anyway, I tell this Fromp lady, if you ain't happy, I'm not happy. Return the car and I'll refund all your money."

"Sounds fair to me," I observed.

"She says 'nothing doing.' She's keeping the cream puff cause it runs and looks good, but I got to give her back $2,500. Not an option. I would have lost money on the deal. I knew I could get what I paid, even with the additional

100,000 miles. Well, I never heard from her again, even though I caught sight of the lady driving around town. The car still runs perfect."

The next morning, I telephoned J.T. Rollins at the office of the Attorney General. After a five-minute bilingual useless recorded message, an equally useless secretary transferred the call.

"J. T. Rollins here." J. T. was a him.

"Mr. Rollins, this is Larry Fox. I'm calling regarding claim #A37-412."

"Just a minute. I'll bring the file up on my screen...Yes, here it is. Who are you?"

"The attorney for Trembly."

"My notes reflect your client sold a car with a rolled-back odometer."

"My client's innocent. He didn't know the odometer was altered."

"That's not my problem. He advertised the car as having low mileage without doing his homework. Maybe somebody else did roll the odometer back, but unless you can prove who it was, at the very least I'm charging your client with false advertising. But I'll tell you what, since I'm a nice guy, I'll give you a couple of weeks to prove to me who the real culprit is. If you do, your guy is off the hook."

What a deal. I do the Attorney General's work, and the Attorney General gets credit for another conviction. In the alternative, Trembly has criminal charges filed against him because the Attorney General is too lazy to conduct a legitimate investigation.

I located "Sassaman Brothers Auto Service" in Freefield, New Jersey. Their address was on the car title they had submitted to the auction company. Someone named Everett Sassaman had sworn before a notary public that at time of title transfer into his name, the 1999 Buick possessed 20,040 miles. I ordered a copy of the prior title. Manny Thurgood sold the car to Sassaman. Thurgood affirmed the Buick had 120,040 miles when he transferred the title.

I contacted the New Jersey Department of Motor Vehicles and ordered copies of the last 50 used car titles transferred by Sassaman to new purchasers. Then I ordered the same 50 titles of the owners who had sold the vehicles to Sassaman. In 36 cases, there were odometer rollbacks of exactly 100,000 miles.

I telephoned the New Jersey Department of Motor Vehicles to advise them of the problem.

"That *is* a problem," Elsie, the motor vehicle title clerk, agreed, "but thankfully it's not *our* office's problem."

"It isn't?"

"Well, I'm no attorney, but it seems that this issue ought to be reported to the proper authorities, don't you think?"

"Elsie, doesn't your office check new license odometer readings against old ones to make sure there aren't any roll-backs?"

"Who has the time? Anyway, it's the notary and the owner who certify to the odometer reading. We just record the information."

I contacted the Roxbury County District Attorney's office as Sassaman Brothers Auto Service was located in Roxbury County. Assistant District Attorney Sally Mehlenberger took my call. I explained the problem.

"So what the hell do you want me to do?" she barked.

The answer seemed rather obvious to me. "Arrest Sassaman," I suggested.

"Just how green are you?" she said.

"I don't understand."

"Look, pal, suppose Sassaman only has five or six mechanics working for him. How am I going to prove who did what - have them hire one of our county detectives as a seventh mechanic to work there half a year until he gains their confidence? That, my friend, is the stuff of movies."

Sassaman was selling cars across state lines. The fraudulent rollback scheme constituted a federal offense. I decided to stop playing with amateurs. I wrote a four-page chronology of the case to my local office of the FBI. I included copies of 50 car titles and their predecessor titles. I noted that 36 of the titles reflected diminutions in odometer readings of exactly 100,000. I requested that the FBI investigate.

Three weeks later I received a call from Special Agent Andrew Peterson of the Federal Bureau of Investigation.

"Are you *Fox* who sent the Bureau a letter?"

I wanted to ask him if he was the agent who read the letter that Fox had sent, but it seemed too Dr. Seussian.

"Yes," I confirmed.

"It's certainly an interesting problem," Peterson observed. (Elsie at the New Jersey Department of Motor Vehicles had offered the same sentiments.)

"Fox..."

"Yes...Peterson?"

"We're experiencing cutbacks."

"Where?"

"Here at the FBI. It's been six months since we hired a new agent. The government's out of money."

"That's a shame."

"Yes, it is. As an example, there are only three agents assigned in this entire district to investigate internal teller bank fraud. If a bank teller steals less than half a million, we 'red list' the teller, and close the investigation. It isn't worth it to prosecute. It's terrorists. Terrorists are the high priority now. Get my drift, Fox?"

I thanked Peterson for his time.

- - - - - - - - - - - - - - - - - - - -

Mrs. Fleegenheim stopped by the office unannounced. The poor dear was 80 years old, and lived entirely on social security.

"You got to help me, Larry." Then she started to shake again. She handed me a certified letter from the 300-lawyer Philadelphia firm retained by her small township to chase down local citizens who had failed for 18 months or more to pay their private residential water and sewer bills.

"I've been in the hospital. Then they sent me to rehab. I never saw the water bill," she explained.

The certified letter noted that her $82.50 billing had gone unpaid. Interest had been added, as had postage and the cost of filing formal legal action. As a result, the small debt had grown exponentially. The law firm of Dunbar, Dinkel, and Farnsworth now sought payment of $973.43, including $8.33 in copy costs.

"What do I do now?" she stammered.

I telephoned Dunbar, Dinkel, and Farnsworth. Attorney Gleeson - a guy who had gone to law school specializing in overdue water bills - took the call.

"There's not much I can do," he explained. "When scofflaws aren't brought to justice, it ultimately affects all of us. If I don't prosecute this claim to the fullest extent of the law, I'll get fired."

That night I slept a little sounder, knowing that even though Sassaman might still be rolling back odometers, at least Trembly and old Mrs. Fleegenheim would soon be off the streets. Maybe the two could share a cell and save the government some cash. Then Uncle Sam could afford to hire one or two more FBI agents.

Chapter 30
The Rollback

CHAPTER 31

LITTLE LAMBY

When death came, the wealthy and powerful Egyptians of old prepared for their final journey by furnishing their tombs with the necessities that would come in handy in the afterlife. Servants, food, gold, and vats of olive oil were but a few of the personal items transported into the next world. Often family histories and works of art also accompanied the deceased.

Joe Pasternak recently passed away. I never met him, but went to the viewing out of respect for his wife, whose sister lived next door to me. There he was, stretched out in the coffin. This was probably the first time he was wearing make-up in public, but that wasn't what caught my eye. Situated next to his right hand was a six-pack of beer, resting right on top of the satin liner. Two mourners in line in front of me also noticed the aluminum pop-top cans, held together with a plastic carry-out strap, for ease of transportation now, or wherever Joe might soon find himself.

"He sure liked his suds!" one drinking buddy observed.

"Yup," the other lush confirmed. "I never saw him without a beer."

Come to think of it, I could make the same boast.

- - - - - - - - - - - - - - - - - - - -

My wife, Teresa, and her sister, Ruthie, had an old spinster aunt, Agnes Tuttle. The two sisters were Tuttle's only living relatives. Since Ruthie lived in Virginia, Aunt Agnes, by default, became Teresa's responsibility.

Teresa never complained. Every day, she looked in on Agnes, who, despite her 87 years, still lived alone in her first floor apartment. The old lady didn't drive and only walked with the assistance of a cane, so Teresa had to shop, make meals, and do laundry for her elderly relative. And there was Whiskers, the cat. Whiskers was 16 years old and suffered from terrible allergies. Teresa had to feed the useless cat as well. When the cat wasn't sleeping, it played with a large red bow that once adorned some forgotten Christmas present.

Taking care of Auntie Agnes was no picnic. She was half blind, couldn't hear very well, and was chronically nasty - not exactly the upbeat type.

One day I helped Teresa drag in a 30-pound bag of scented cat litter. She cleaned some dishes while I changed the water in the damn cat's bowl. We both noticed the new arrival as we prepared to leave. There, sitting on the fake fireplace mantel, its knees crossed, its arms folded, its black button eyes smiling, its brown triangular fuzzy nose accentuating a delicate red tongue, reposed a petite pure white stuffed toy lamb. It was smiling slightly. Teresa walked across the sitting room to perform a closer inspection. It was love at first sight. I don't think she had ever looked at me quite the same way.

"What a precious little creature," she observed, as she stroked the fluffy knotted fur.

"You say something?" agitated Agnes inquired, as she sat on the big couch in her nightie, with her self-imposed 7:00 p.m. bedtime curfew rapidly approaching.

"Where did this precious dear come from?"

Agnes opened her good eye slightly. "That's Little Lamby. The neighbor upstairs gave her to me last week so I don't get lonely. Sometimes the cat hides for awhile. Little Lamby always stays put."

And so it was that we made Little Lamby's acquaintance. We walked Agnes into her bedroom, tucked her in, and turned out the light. It was time to leave.

"Wait a minute," Agnes called out. "Bring Little Lamby in here."

Teresa delicately lifted the stuffed toy from its perch, straightened Little Lamby's legs, and laid the lamb next to

Agnes, who smiled for the first time in a month. Little Lamby had that effect on people.

From that day on, Little Lamby slept with Agnes. During the day, the lamb sat on the edge of the bed, its legs crossed, its arms folded. Ultimately, when Agnes contracted pneumonia two months later, Little Lamby never left her side.

The end was near, so we brought in round-the-clock nurses. Agnes wanted to die at home. Ruthie came up from Virginia just in time. Three days later, Agnes was dead. The two sisters made funeral arrangements, and then straightened up the apartment.

"Isn't it something how during the last few days, Aunt Agnes never let Little Lamby out of her sight," Ruthie mused.

Teresa nodded her head up and down, as she stared at the snow-white lamb now once again reclining on the sitting room mantel.

"You know," Ruthie began, "I've been thinking..."

"What about?"

"Little Lamby..."

"What about Little Lamby?"

"Aunt Agnes sure loved that stuffed lamb..."

"Uh huh..."

"I was thinking, when we have the viewing tomorrow, Little Lamby ought to be in the coffin with Agnes. They belong together when Agnes goes to her last reward. I'm sure you agree, Teresa."

- - - - - - - - - - - - - - - - - - -

That night, Teresa and I went to bed early. We would need our strength for the morning viewing, afternoon funeral, and family dinner. I dosed off by 10:00 p.m. with Teresa by my side.

Someone was crying...I heard pacing...downstairs. I turned on the night light. It was 2:00 a.m. It was Teresa downstairs. I made my way to the situs of the lamentation.

Teresa was sitting at the kitchen table, her eyes swollen and red. A pile of discarded tissues lay in a clump.

"Is there something wrong?" I used my most understanding 2:00 a.m. voice.

"No." She blew her nose again.

"Good. Then we can go back to bed."

"It's Little Lamby!"

"Who?" I inquired in my 'men are from Mars, women are from Venus' voice.

"The dear little lamb."

"What dear little...you mean Agnes' stuffed toy? Is that what we're talking about?"

"I saw a documentary on TV last month about burials..."

"Now Teresa, we've all got to die sometime..."

"Let me finish. After you're buried, you begin to mummify. Your skin turns to leather, your eyes sink in their sockets, and ...and it's awful..."

"Teresa, I know you loved your aunt, but really dear, she already looked like that. There isn't much you can do..."

"Listen...let me finish! Ruthie wants to bury sweet Little Lamby with decrepit Agnes. I've just got to save that lamb from a fate worse than death. Little Lamby shouldn't be forced to sit there for a couple of centuries watching Agnes turn into a ghoul."

My lifemate was in terrible pain. I wasn't quite sure why, but that was not at this particular moment a relevant issue. What she needed was for me to say just the right thing, *even if I was clueless.*

"Dear..."

"What?"

"We need to rescue Little Lamby. We better do it now."

Teresa raised her head from the pile of tissues and looked at me in a way I had never before observed. A radiant glow instantly spread from her cheeks. She had never appeared so beautiful.

"I'll get dressed," she whispered.

We drove to Aunt Agnes' apartment. Whiskers met us at the door even though it was 2:45 in the morning. Little Lamby was sitting on the edge of the bed. Teresa gently lifted the fuzzy toy, tenderly kissed the creature's cheeks and carefully placed the stuffed lamb in a shopping bag. Then she turned to leave.

"Wait a minute," I said. "Where's the red ribbon the cat always plays with?"

Teresa soon found it under the refrigerator. I put the ribbon on the bed where Little Lamby had been perched.

"O.K. Let's make our get away," I said.

- - - - - - - - - - - - - - - - - - -

The viewing was at 10:00 a.m. at the funeral home. With just minutes to go, Ruthie was nowhere to be found.

"She may have overslept at the hotel," I suggested to Teresa.

At 9:58, Ruthie charged into the mortuary parlor.

"Sorry I'm late," she puffed, "but I ran over to Agnes' apartment this morning to get the lamb. The damned cat...he leaves his stupid ribbon where Little Lamby was, and took her away. I looked everywhere, even under the refrigerator. I guess Agnes will just have to be buried without Little Lamby."

An hour later, Agnes was lowered into the ground. Her best friend, Little Lamby, missed the service and interment. She was sitting on the shelf in our hall closet, her legs crossed, her arms folded, a slight smile on her face.

Chapter 31
Little Lamby

CHAPTER 32

NINE-TENTHS

One of my favorite subjects in school was Greek and Roman mythology. These stories about the omnipotent gods who lived on Mount Olympus, in the Mediterranean Sea, and elsewhere, gave rise to great temples and even greater literary masterpieces.

It is indeed the rare law school professor who has offered a course on the mythology of the law - the study of the legends that have, for centuries, floated in and out of courthouses. No one knows from what ancient bards these tales may have originated, but similar to Greek and Roman mythology, true believers have often used the stories to construct their own temples to the god of Justice.

- - - - - - - - - - - - - - - - - - -

"Charlie Bibbelputz is calling," my secretary announced.

I froze for an instant and quickly reviewed my mental archives of nut-case clients. "Isn't he the guy who tried to sue the liquid oxygen company for stealing the air he breathes?"

"That's the one," Cathy confirmed as she politely smiled and quickly shut her door.

I picked up the phone.

"Hi, Mr. Bibbelputz." I tried to sound enthusiastic.

"Listen, I have a quick question."

I've been practicing law for more than 30 years. Not one client has ever called with a *slow* question, the type of protracted inquiry for which a lawyer might legitimately send a bill.

"You do?"

"Yeah. See it's like this. The First National Bank kinda made a mistake."

"Kinda? Mistake?"

"Yeah. They seem to have credited my checking account with more money than I deposited last week. Can I keep it?"

"How much of a mistake?"

"I gave the teller 10 bucks. She entered $10,000. Can I write a check and buy a car or something?"

"Mr. Bibbelputz..."

"What?"

"Suppose the shoe were on the other foot. Suppose you had entrusted the bank with $10,000, and the teller entered the deposit as only $10. Would you expect the bank to correct the error?"

"Of course, but that's because the bank already has lots of money. I don't. Before this stroke of luck, my checking account never had more than $70 in it. I sure could use the extra cash."

This was no longer a quick question at all, and Bibbelputz was no longer a client seeking advice. He had received an answer with which he disagreed, and now he wanted to engage in a debate.

"Listen, Counsellor, someone told me I can keep the money, 'cause possession is nine-tenths of the law. Ain't that so?"

One of the great myths of the law - almost as good as the myth that when someone dies without a last will, everything goes to the state. Or, the myth that if you transfer all of grandma's assets out of her name, including title to her house, you can dump the old bag of bones in the nearest nursing home and she won't have to pay for services rendered.

Possession is nine-tenths of the law - what exactly does that mean? What ever happened to the other missing tenth?

"Mr. Bibbelputz..."

"What?"

"Was the *someone* who told you that nonsense an attorney?"

"I don't think so."

"Then the advice you got was worth what you paid for it."

"I don't get it."

"It means you better tell the bank that it made a mistake, so it can retrieve its money."

"Are you sure?"

"I'm sure that if you spend the money, you'll be spending your next vacation in the federal pen."

- - - - - - - - - - - - - - - - - - - -

It had been a tough week. I had probably answered 60 or 70 *quick* questions. I needed a slow relaxing dinner with my wife. We drove over to the "Villa Stuffo," our favorite Italian restaurant. Our enthusiasm for the eatery was shared Valley-wide. The place was packed. People were standing outside in the pale August twilight, waiting for their names to crackle over the parking lot loudspeaker.

Ultimately we were seated in a romantic booth near the glowing fish tanks.

"Would-a you-a like-a some-a wine-a wid-a your-a meal-a?" the waiter asked.

We both declined but ordered our favorite, chicken cacciatore. We munched on bread sticks, sipped minestrone soup, and watched the multi-colored fish effortlessly glide from one end of the tank to the other. I began to relax for the first time all week.

The waiter brought our entrees. The aroma smelled heavenly.

"Would-a you-a like-a some-a extra-a cheeze-a?"

"Yes," my wife confirmed as we smiled at each other. The long wait had been worth it. The waiter grated, bowed, and vanished.

I took a first bite. Life was good.

"Pardon-a me-a," the voice said.

I looked up. It was the maître d'.

"Yes?"

"You-a must-a leave right-a now-a. I-a so-a sorry."

"What?"

"De-a restaurant-a, she's on-a de fire. Everyone must-a, how-a you say-a, evacuate-a."

Two firemen in full uniform were giving the same news to other startled patrons at neighboring booths. I began to smell smoke, which prompted my memory to harken back to Coast Guard fire school training. I grabbed my wife, kept our heads low, and tried not to panic. We quickly found an emergency exit, and scampered to the parking lot.

The scene looked like a disaster movie. There were several gigantic hook-and-ladder trucks, water hoses all over the ground, red flashing lights and scores of fire fighters, some carrying axes. We made our way in all this confusion back to our car, which was impounded by a mass of fire and safety equipment.

My wife and I stood arm-in-arm, in the romantic August night, the light of a full moon cascading upon us. We waited in fear for the restaurant to go up in flames. We waited for clouds of smoke to billow out of broken windows.

It was then we began to notice a most unusual sight. Patrons, perhaps more than a hundred, had, similar to us, found their way back to their trapped vehicles. But, clearly, none of them had attended Coast Guard fire school. On their way out, they had tarried just long enough to gather up the food, drink, complimentary garlic bread, and utensils from their tables. They had now spread these temporarily interrupted feasts on car hoods and truck tailgates. The couple in the Chevy next to us had even snatched the flickering candle centerpiece, which was still lit.

"What, no food?" he called out incredulously as he and his companion sat together on their back bumper. They balanced their plates of eggplant parmigiana on their laps. His napkin dangled from his open shirt collar.

"No," I replied. "They said the place was on fire, so we ran for our lives."

"There's no fire," my new friend explained as he wolfed down another sumptuous mouthful. "Some idiot

215

tried to sneak a cigarette in the men's room, and threw the butt in the wastebasket. It was just a few smoldering hand towels."

I looked out upon the moonlit parking lot. Everyone was eating, except my wife and me. An announcement came over the loudspeaker.

"Lady-a and-a gentleman-a. We-a soooo sorry-a for-a de-a inconvenience-a. No-a charge-a tonight-a for-a your-a dinners-a."

"You're damn right," our parking lot neighbor agreed, as fragments of eggplant fell from his mouth.

"I wasn't going to pay for a fire-damaged meal. And this candle centerpiece? It's mine, 'cause possession is nine-tenths of the law. Any lawyer'll tell you that."

Chapter 32
Nine-tenths

CHAPTER 33

THE DEATH WISH

In the movie, "Death Wish," hero-villain Charles Bronson vows to set things right. When members of his family are brutalized by ruthless thugs, something inside Bronson snaps. The glacial speed of the legal system, with its frustrating and burdensome procedural technicalities, has failed him. Probable cause? Evidence? Arrest warrant? Bronson don't need no stinkin' grand jury indictment to nail the bad guys. And so he stalks the streets of the metropolis at night, armed only with a sense of justice and his .357 magnum.

Throughout the film, various nogoodnicks try to commit mayhem upon innocent-looking Bronson. Some ask him for his wallet; others push him in a puddle. Once accosted, Bronson, the meek victimized citizen, becomes, in the blink of a vigilante eye, Mr. Judge-Jury-and-Executioner. He pulls out his hidden handgun, and proceeds to dispatch every wrongdoer in sight.

At the conclusion of each evening's entrapment, he returns to his home for some milk, cookies, and a well-deserved rest. The movie has just seven sequels, because the metropolis finally runs out of criminals. So Bronson moves to another city to take up his crusade anew. Unlike Alexander the Great, he has more worlds to conquer.

It would be such fun to be Bronson, if only for a day or two. If anyone dared kick dirt in my face, there'd be hell to pay.

- - - - - - - - - - - - - - - - - - -

What about that trucker with the tattoo of a naked lady on his arm? Why must he thrust his 18-wheel rig to within 10 feet of my rear on a 6-lane highway? I'm doing the speed limit, and he has plenty of room to pass. Maybe he enjoys the rush of intimidating a defenseless motorist in a compact car underpowered by a mere four cylinders. I take my foot off the accelerator and motion for him to pass. Instead he now maneuvers to within just five feet of my bumper. All I can see in my rear view mirror are the chrome strips of a radiator grill. There's only one thing to do. I reach into the holster conveniently dangling from the right door handle, and pull out my constant companion, a .357 magnum. I set the car to cruise control, roll down the window and peering backwards, stick my head into the torrent of air passing by at 52 mph. Carefully taking aim, I shoot out both of the big bruiser's front tires. Then I look in my rear view mirror to see if justice has prevailed.

The truck swerves at a dramatic 90° angle, and begins to disappear in a ball of flames as it flips over and over, landing on top of a guardrail.

"I guess he'll think twice before he pulls a stunt like that again," I muse to myself as I blow away the smoke from the gun barrel and place the equalizer back into its holster.

There are a couple of problems with my fantasy. First, I don't own a .357 magnum. Second, I live and work in a very small town. Everyone knows me, or his or her secretary knows my third cousin. Charles Bronson could come and go in Metropolis undetected. And most of the people he slaughtered didn't have secretaries, nor, we presume, families.

I'm stuck. I have to be nice. Pleasant, actually. To step on a toe, to burn a bridge in this community is professional suicide. The IRS auditor going through my accounts receivable has a sister engaged to the son of my best client. I smile as I hand him the next box of ledger sheets.

- - - - - - - - - - - - - - - - - - - -

It had been a difficult day. The Zeismonger file was missing. I looked under "Z" in the filing cabinet. Then I looked on the floor under my desk. Goose egg.

The plumber finally showed up to inspect the two-day-old stagnant fluid in the basement. "I think there's a tree root growing in the main stack," he surmised.

I didn't even know I owned a "stack."

"It's a city tree," I argued. "They planted it along *their* street."

"Yeah," he agreed, "but them roots is on *your* side of the sidewalk. Read the ordinance."

"Larry..." My secretary was calling from the top of the basement steps.

"What?"

"You're going to be late for the Zeismonger settlement over at Attorney Killroy's office."

I could feel my blood pressure escalating. I was holding up a house sale, I didn't know where the file was, and the plumber had that unmistakable gleam in his eye as if I were about to unintentionally subsidize his kid's college education.

"We may have to dig down to where your lateral connects with the street," the plumber theorized.

"How far is that?"

"Maybe 16...maybe 18 feet below. It's all based on gravity flow."

My future happiness rested in part on the unrestricted ooze of human effluent. I decided to go to the Zeismonger settlement with or without the file. If I didn't make some money fast, I'd have to rent a portable toilet for my support staff.

I jumped in my car, the car with four cylinders and no .357 magnum. Attorney Killroy's office was about 10 blocks away. If I didn't get delayed by traffic, I'd only be 5 or 10 minutes late.

By ignoring several ordinances applicable to the operation of a motor vehicle, I succeeded in getting across town in a timely manner. Killroy was located near New and Market Streets, where everyone jockeyed for scarce metered parking spaces.

By a stroke of luck, a space appeared just half a block ahead on my side of the street. It no longer mattered that it was 92 degrees outside, that the conditioner dispensed cold air out of just one vent - on the passenger side, nor that my plumber might have to dig to China. At least I had a place to park. I pulled one space ahead, put my car in reverse, and prepared to back into the space. Life wasn't so bad after all. That's right. There was even some time left on the meter.

Then it happened. As I looked in my rear view mirror, a girl, all of 17, smacking gum and talking on her cell phone, drove her mini-crap-something - maybe an old Beetle - to within 5 feet of my back bumper. Then she cut hard to the right and zipped into *my* space. She was still talking, smacking, and popping as she alighted from her vehicle.

Never had I been so violated. A sense of rage displaced my usual "Larry" demeanor. Veins bulged in my forehead. I was so blinded by injustice that I failed to note the presence of an elderly man sitting in the car parked parallel to mine to the right. Because of the heat, his car windows were rolled down as well.

"YOU GODDAMNED BITCH" I heard some unknown demon from within me scream at the girl whose image I now caught in my rear view mirror.

The old man sat straight up in his seat, and turned his shaken face toward me. He knew a Charles Bronson when he saw one. I probably had a .357 hidden in my car.

"Sorry!" he exclaimed. "Take the space, with my compliments. Just pull ahead and let me get the hell outta here."

I was embarrassed by my inappropriate outburst, but there was no time to reflect and apologize. The old man was gone in an instant, so I transitioned into the newly vacated space.

After I clean up the criminal element in this town, I just might take up my crusade in another location.

Chapter 33
The Death Wish

CHAPTER 34

THE BUDGETARY CRISIS

There is a cheap, almost useless type of paper that was designed to perform only one function - retard the slippage of flesh. It comes on huge, unending spools, and is used by two similar professions.

The butcher at the nearby farmer's market has a role about the size of a Volkswagen suspended by chains attached to the I-beams supporting his roof.

"I'd like a quarter pound of sliced bacon, please."

"You got it, Mr. Fox," Burt the butcher assures me. He has more hair on his back than I have on my head. Why he allows paying customers to see this is beyond me.

He slices my order with amazing dexterity and speed acquired from years behind the meat counter. Then, without looking up, he deftly reaches into the air, grasps the loose leading edge of the mammoth paper roll, and tears off just the right amount for next week's breakfast.

By the time I get home, some of the bacon grease has begun to ooze through its cheap protective covering. But that's the way it is. The paper was only designed to retard the bacon from slipping about in its packaging. Wax paper may not leak, but it's more expensive and, worse, leaves wax particles in the food. Butcher paper has survived the test of time.

There's one other profession that uses such paper to retard the slippage of flesh.

"Well, just put your underpants ober der. Now, Mr. Fox, hop up on de examination table."

"I'm a Fox, not a bunny," I correct Dr. Abissinus, the proctologist.

"Wery funny," he assures me with an accompanying smile that I can't see, since my derriere is now being elevated toward the ceiling. But that's O.K. I won't fall, because my naked flesh now clings like bacon to the cheap paper covering the exam table. The good doctor must have a roll of it the size of a Volkswagen hidden under the comfy headrest with the convenient hole for my face. After he's done with me, an 18-year-old nurse's assistant laying in wait yanks on the end of the big spool and covers the table once again. Then she glances at me with a snicker and walks out the door.

- - - - - - - - - - - - - - - - - - - -

County council met the second Tuesday night of each month. These important elected officials were tasked both with the responsibility of overseeing the county budget, and with monitoring expenditures for the public good.

It was time to review the county's financial health for the next fiscal year. The patient didn't look well. Initial estimates suggested that projected income from taxes might not equal proposed expenditures. How would a paltry $67 million operate the courthouse, the jail, the home for the aged, and maintain all the county roads and bridges?

I represented several courthouse employees. There was a rumor circulating that hours might be cut or jobs eliminated. I joined a large crowd of anxious spectators as they flooded the fourth floor council chambers.

The president of council addressed the sea of nervous faces. He was very important. I knew this because he arrived in a chauffeur-driven limo that was parked in his reserved space near the courthouse entrance.

"Ladies and gentlemen," he began, "we need to find new ways to streamline next year's budget. Government waste must stop. We must all pull our belts a little tighter. We owe it to the taxpayers of this great county."

The President was good to his word. With the help of his crack team of eight administrative assistants, they put their heads together and began to cut the fat from the budget. Those who worked at the courthouse, the jail, and the nursing home would just have to learn to sacrifice.

The water cooler in the Recorder of Deeds office was missing. It was probably being repaired. I went up to the Prothonotary's office on the second floor. Funny. No water cooler there, either. I stood for a moment scratching my chin.

"Haven't you heard?" Lydia called out from behind her work station.

"Heard what?" I responded.

"They took the coolers."

"Who's 'they'?"

"County council. It's all explained in this memo we just got." Lydia handed me an official-looking document.

The calculations were indisputable. I read them over lunch with several thirsty courthouse staffers. With the removal of all 18 courthouse water coolers, the county bean-counters projected an annual savings of almost $2,700, or a deduction of nearly 4 cents from every landowner's tax bill. At first blush, this might have seemed insignificant, until one realized that similar cost cutting had occurred at the prison and the county old age home. If the wheelchair-bound octogenarians at the county home could be expected to rise from their mobile seating to imbibe from the hallway drinking fountains, the least the able-bodied courthouse employees could do would be to join in the countywide sacrifice.

It was time for lunch. I took a bite from my courthouse cafeteria tuna sandwich, which could have passed for chicken or ham salad, and then walked over to the drinking fountain at the far end of the wall. Soon I returned to the table and my friends.

"You didn't just drink the municipal water, did you?" Lee, the title searcher, asked. "I've lived in this city all my life, but I've never done that!"

"That water is sucked from the Delaware River below the sewage treatment plant," Carol from the assessment office advised me. "They say the water has been 'treated,' but who knows what that means?"

In 20 minutes, I was as sick as a dog. I burst into the first floor bathroom and sat in the stall. Funny. The toilet paper dispenser with the soft white scented tissue was gone. It had been there for years. In its place was a spool of paper, suspended from a lone wire. It was the type of paper used to wrap bacon.

The county bean-counters had come up with another way to save money. I had not complained when they decided to install the little cameras in the urinals that activated the flushing mechanism as I stepped back. Over the years, my expectations of privacy have decreased as the unauthorized distribution of my social security number has increased. But this newest toilet stall indignity was the last straw.

It was time to leave my seat, as it were, and take a stand. I headed for the fourth floor county council president's office. It was time to tell him exactly what I thought about his...

Uh oh! First, I needed to visit the bathroom again. The combination of tuna surprise and sewage treatment water took precedence. I ran into the hallway lav next to the presidential office suite, and sat down. Funny. A dispenser of white fluffy scented tissue reposed on the stall wall. Apparently budgetary constraints hadn't made their way up to the fourth floor.

A few minutes later, I walked into the president's plushly carpeted office, and stood next to the natural spring water cooler upon which the chauffeur was leaning. I waited for the assistant receptionist to look up from the latest issue of *Vogue*. I asked to see a representative from county council.

"No one's here," the young maiden responded.

"When will they return?"

"Don't know. Everyone flew to Vegas for a convention on how to save money. Why don't you try back next week?

Chapter 34
The Budgetary Crisis

227

CHAPTER 35

RESTITUTION

Every criminal defense counsel has his or her favorite *I-have-represented-the-dumbest-felon-in-the-entire-world* story. Over the years, some of these misadventures have been reported by the various media. Like the bank robber who gave the quaking teller a demand note written on his own letterhead. Or the mastermind who, during a high-speed chase with the cops, remembered what his driving instructor had taught him, and signaled each time he changed lanes or made a turn. One of my favorite tales deals with the house burglar who tried to elude his pursuers in the midnight darkness of a woods, but to no avail, because he was wearing sneakers that activated blinking red lights each time he took a step.

It was criminal court week at the Northampton County Courthouse. I joined a couple of other defense counsel in the cafeteria for an unscheduled informal breakfast before we headed upstairs to face another day of nervous clients, wide-eyed jurors, arrogant assistant district attorneys, and wise-as-owls judges.

"My jury's still out," Gary Ungerleider offered, though he seemed more interested in the morning paper.

"What's the charge?" Hughy Hambrook inquired.

I liked Gary and Hughy. They were both competent and energetic, and when the assistant district attorneys got sloppy or overestimated the strength of their cases, these fellow public defenders could plant the seed of reasonable doubt in a jury's mind, causing the scales of justice to sway unexpectedly in the other direction.

"Aggravated assault. My guy stabbed the victim 17 times," Gary explained.

"And the vic lived?" Hughy asked.

"Yup!"

"What's your defense? That the knife was dull?" Gary joked.

Gary took an oversized bite out of a Boston Creme donut and turned to me. "You got anything going today?" he asked.

"A hearing this morning before Judge Garbel. I'm trying to get a three-year prison sentence to include immediate work release based upon the fact that my client is the dumbest human being alive."

"Sounds like a good defense," Gary assured me. "If I were the judge, both you and your client would get high marks for creativity."

"What did he do?" Hughy asked.

"Stole a million dollars."

"Million, huh? Not bad," said Hughy. "How did this clown ever qualify for a free public defender?"

"Actually, he's broke," I explained. "He had to give the loot back, but some of it is still missing."

"That's the down side of theft," Gary interjected. "Sometimes you get caught."

"He can't be all that dumb, if he made off with a million bucks," Hughy reasoned.

"You may change your mind after you hear this story," I suggested.

True defense counsel never miss an opportunity to study the criminal mind or the lack thereof. Hughy took a last sip of coffee. Gary wolfed down the remainder of the Boston Creme. The floor was mine.

"I represent Oliver Pinkel."

"Flag on the play," Gary interrupted. "No way is that his real name."

"You want to hear this story or not?"

"O.K. Fine. I'm buying it. Go on," Gary assured me.

"Oliver Pinkel. Door-to-door vacuum cleaner salesman."

Gary muffled a laugh. Hughy just shook his head.

"I know. But it gets better. See, he was having trouble making ends meet. That's when, by a stroke of luck, he learned his elderly and frail great aunt, who suffered from dementia and senility, had taken up residence in a nursing home just past Kintnersville. Although they had never met, Oliver decided to drop in for a visit. It was the least he could do.

"Rumor had it that dear old Auntie's will directed that everything she had - and it was a ton - go to the local animal shelter. Resourceful Oliver thought he could put the money to better use.

"So...he starts logging in a visit every Sunday, and two months later, he walked away with a general Power of Attorney, authorizing him to manage Auntie's liquid assets. The vacuum biz must have picked up, because soon he was seen driving a new Rolls to all of his sales calls. At the same time, the great aunt's checks to the nursing home began to bounce. Oliver, now on a world tour, found that his busy schedule precluded him from looking in on his charge or paying her bills.

"He finally gets caught?" Hughy surmised.

"Exactly. Had to sell the new house he just bought at the Jersey shore, return the Rolls, and account for his other acquisitions, including a diamond-studded Rolex. Unfortunately, the limo had depreciated, and the world tour had been costly. Oliver came up short about $400,000, so the judge threw him in jail."

"Imagine that," Gary sympathized.

"So, what makes this jerk the dumbest guy on earth?" Hughy asked.

"The rumor at the nursing home about the cash going to the animal shelter was just that - a rumor. Turns out Auntie never did write a last will and testament."

Gary looked at Hughy. Hughy looked at Gary. Then they both burst out laughing. Gary was the first to speak.

"You're kidding me, right?"

"It gets better. Not only is Oliver auntie's closest living relative - he's her *only* living relative. She died two months later. Her entire fortune goes to you-know-who."

"The bastard stole his *own* money - *and* went to jail for it!" Gary laughed. "Classic!"

"Of course, part of the judge's sentence is that Oliver pay restitution to his aunt's estate, since inheritance tax is due," I explained. "But suffice it to say, he's broke. I'm trying to get him out on work release. Twenty or 30 thousand vacuum cleaners ought to do it."

Chapter 35
Restitution

CHAPTER 36

GOOD-BYE

I have always tried to maintain a positive attitude. Why not look on the bright side? Doctors take the opposite approach. When tests are negative, they think things are good.

I remember when Dr. Branigan gave me the news out in the hallway. Mom had the Big C. I thanked him for his concern, as I lightly knocked on her hospital room door.

"Who is it? Friend or enema?"

Mom, the comedienne, was awake, so I walked in.

There were several intravenous lines running from the computer-pump-monitor into her arm. A urine bag hung at bedside near the floor. She didn't appear to be negative about the positive diagnosis.

"They gave me a colostomy bag, see?" She lifted the bed sheet with her free arm.

"Yes."

"It's amazing. Now I can take a dump any place, anytime I want and no one will be the wiser. I should have had one of these installed years ago when pay toilets were all the rage."

"Are you in any pain?" I asked.

"A little. But it's worth it. This is the first time I've ever owned a bag that matches my shoes."

With so little time left, she was still able to teach me invaluable lessons on humor and dignity in the face of death.

- - - - - - - - - - - - - - - - - -

A year later it was Dad's turn to impart one final lesson. He looked so small as he lay unconscious in the bed with the raised aluminum side rails. Two attentive nurses connected some more machinery as they engaged in an animated pre-lunch discussion:

"No. Every day you want the same food. Why not eat something different?"

"But they have the best French - "

"I don't care, Sally. It's time for a change, like Wendy's, or KFC, or maybe Pizza Hut."

Two days later, much to everyone's surprise, Dad awoke from three days of unconsciousness. The doctor asked me if Dad preferred to die at home. I quickly made the arrangements to discharge him from the hospital. I still don't know what was more difficult: locating his glasses, hearing aid, teeth, watch, and slippers, or attempting to attach them to different parts of his body. It was like trying to create a sculpture with jello. I slowly sat him up as I buttoned his shirt.

"We're going home, Dad."

"Not yet," he corrected me.

"Sure we are. The doctor said you can."

"Take me to Burger King."

No one knew Dad better than I. In his 78 years, he had never once eaten at a fast-food franchise. He had never consumed a single Mc-Anything. Three days in a coma had clearly left my father delusional.

"Dad, I'm going to take you home now, O.K.?"

"No. Take me to Burger King. I heard they have the best French fries. Light on the grease, just a hint of salt."

I stared in disbelief. Who was this impostor in my father's pajamas?

"Dad, let me take you home. Then I'll drive over to Burger King, and get you some French fries to eat in your bedroom."

"It won't be the same. They're best eaten hot."

"Who told you that?"

"Does it matter? I think it was a nurse."

"Dad, you're too weak to make the trip all the way across town."

"Son, if you were dying and had one last wish to eat French fries right at the drive-in window, I'd take *you* there."

I bundled Dad in my car. We drove across town to Burger King. I got in the drive-thru lane and placed the order.

"Get a large, son. I'll pay you back later."

I proceeded to the next window, secured a large bag of greasy potato fragments, a small Coke, and turned to my desperately weak father.

"Do you want me to hold the bag?"

"Nope. I can do it." The artistic hands that had held countless violas now cradled their first bag of French fries. He pulled out a golden stick and consumed it. Then he ate another and another. Similar to a chain-smoker, before the remnants of one tender morsel had disappeared, the next was making its way toward his face. He shoved French fries non-stop into his mouth during the 15-minute ride home. Only when the bag was empty did he take a sip of Coke. We parked in the driveway.

"She was right."

"Who?"

"The nurse."

I carried Dad into the house. He never ate again. He lapsed into unconsciousness that night and died the next morning.

- - - - - - - - - - - - - - - - - - - -

Mr. Clangmore was waiting to see me in the conference room - something about suing over property damage.

I didn't have to attend medical school to recognize "the look." This poor soul was near death, although he might not yet have reached his 60th birthday.

"How may I help you?" I asked the pasty gray face.

"A year ago, my neighbor backed his truck into my mailbox, causing $75 in damage. I told him to pay up. He said something about deductibles and how his insurance wouldn't cover it, and to this very day I'm still out the dough. I want you to sue him before it's too late."

"I'm not sure I - "

"I have cancer and I don't have much time left. If I don't get my money now, I may never see it."

Clangmore had a week or two - possibly three. It was remarkable he wanted to spend any of his few remaining hours in small claims court harassing a neighbor.

"I don't want your case, Mr. Clangmore."

"What do you mean?" he stammered. "I'll pay up front."

I escorted him to the door and pointed him toward the nearest Burger King.

Chapter 36
Good-bye

237

CHAPTER 37

REAGAN AND THE ORANGE PUSSYCAT

It was July of 1986. Our nation was about to celebrate the 100th birthday of the Statue of Liberty. For a couple of weeks, I was ordered to abandon the law office and join my Coast Guard Reserve Unit at our New York City Headquarters located at Fort Jay on Governors Island. The island, situated in New York Harbor less than a mile from the Statue, was home to several hundred Coasties and their families. One could only reach the island by ferry, and only if the passenger were associated with the Coast Guard. Those inhabiting this one-kilometer in length outcropping next to the mayhem of downtown Manhattan enjoyed a quiet and secure military lifestyle. No one locked his door. Coasties don't steal from Coasties.

The island had everything a sailor's family might need. A bank, a Burger King, a church, a synagogue, a movie theater, an elementary school, ancient black powder cannon protecting the harbor, an airstrip built during World War I, and Coast Guard buildings of every description.

Everyone there had fought hard to join this, the smallest branch of the military, and so morale was high. Each morning precisely at 8:00, "colors" would sound, and this entire patriotic community would come to a standstill as the flag was raised. The same observance formally ended the day as the flag was secured.

Six stately mansions sat in a neat row on the island, reminders of a grand era now shrouded in history. Each edifice was constructed in identical fashion to the other. Each could have passed for the master's house on a southern plantation. Expansive white columns shot skyward to support an overstated front portico that accentuated a grand double door entrance into each Georgian-style brick and stone castle. These spectacular residences now served as the living quarters for the six admirals billeted on the cozy island.

"Admirals' Row," to which it was commonly referred, looked out upon a manicured parade ground that would have been the pride of any exclusive country club maintenance crew. Three acres of velvet-soft grass, fashioned in a rectangle, gave the admirals' mansions the appearance of opulence only displayed at European palaces. It was at this hallowed place that President Ronald Reagan and Nancy, his wife, were scheduled to address the troops, prior to attending the gala centennial celebration with other dignitaries arriving hourly from around the globe.

The Coast Guard served as host of these internationally televised festivities. Nothing could be left to chance. Nothing could go wrong. More than 2,000 Coasties had been assigned to guard and protect the President during his stay at our facility.

For three days prior to his arrival, we polished our belt buckles, shined our shoes, and patrolled the harbor for terrorists. A sense of pride and excitement filled the air. The sightings of VIPs alighting hourly from the ferry became almost commonplace. Sinatra with the President of France. And there was Liz Taylor, mixing it up with a glum Henry Kissinger. Walter Cronkite was gesturing to Cher. It was as if I were viewing a satirical comedic illustration from Mad Magazine, but these were the real McCoys.

Then, *they* arrived; The Secret Service. They flew in on eight jet-powered camouflaged fly-in-tight-formation helicopters. Eighty Dick Tracy types stepped out on cue onto the parade grounds, each unsmiling governmental servant dressed in a tailor-made suit, each presidential protector carrying a small suitcase.

Within hours of their presence on the island, *things* began to happen. There appeared a mysterious red line, painted on the ground along the water's edge encircling the entire island. We were all called into the assembly hall for a briefing.

"That's the temporary 'kill zone'," the captain explained to 2,000 sailors. "If you cross over the red line, the Secret Service will neutralize you."

"My vet did that to our dog," the boatswain's mate sitting next to me whispered. "After that, 'ol Bruiser sure did watch his step."

I soon learned that those small suitcases didn't contain a change of socks and underwear. These guys were carrying uzis and enough ammo to storm the Bastille. Sharphooters began to appear on rooftops, on the mess deck, and in the security clearance room. They never talked to us; they just grunted into little buttons on their lapels. Each had an earphone with a wire that disappeared into his pressed white shirt collar.

It was time for Reagan and his entourage to make an appearance. So, they lined up 2,000 of us with 2,000 polished belt buckles and 4,000 spit-shined shoes. We stood at attention on the parade grounds, facing Admirals' Row. Then the ground began to shake as three helicopters, each powered by two jet engines, landed just 100 yards away. The Honor Guard began to play *Hail to the Chief* and out stepped President Reagan. Everyone saluted, except the two Secret Service guys standing directly behind me. One of them was talking to a sharpshooter on a nearby roof.

It was a day designed for a birthday party, even if the guest of honor was a century old. The bright sunlight made us more handsome than we actually were. The light harbor breezes reminded us that the ocean, the magnet that had first drawn us to the Coast Guard, reposed nearby. The red, white, and blue flag fluttered above our heads as we waited for the Presidential address.

I was not the only creature who sought to soak in the magic of this fleeting moment in history. The screen door serving the second mansion on the left opened slightly, as an orange cat squeezed through the narrow opening it had created, and made an appearance on the front porch. The feline wore a large red bow around its neck, perhaps in honor of the President's arrival. The cat squinted at the 2,000 sailors, three jet helicopters, 80 Secret Servicemen with uzis, the President and his entourage, and decided to take a little stroll. It sauntered down the stone staircase, across the pedestrian footpath, and entered the manicured parade grounds. This would be the only cat attending the President's speech. The honor guard stopped playing. We all stopped saluting.

Reagan stepped up to the microphone. "Men and women of the United States Coast Guard, I sincerely thank you for making me feel so..."

The cat now approached to within 50 feet of where I stood at ram rod-straight attention. 1,999 other Coasties in 20 symmetrical rows maintained similar postures. After all, the President was talking. The orange cat could not have cared less. He dined on a regular basis with admirals. Reagan had only achieved the rank of lieutenant in the Army Air Corps. It was obvious this cat had its own agenda.

"When I look out among you splendid sailors, I am reminded of..."

The orange cat trotted to a storm sewer grate and began to sniff about. It appeared the animal had found familiar territory and was engaging in a familiar ritual.

"My fellow Americans, without a strong military, we cannot hope to..."

The cat stuck its head through the grate, swished its tail back and forth, and disappeared down the sewer. Perhaps there was a mouse breakfast in the near future.

"You see that, Ted?" The Secret Service guys lurking behind me were actually speaking.

"Yeah. I know," the first motioned to the second. "The cat had something tied around its neck."

Pause.

"Heads you go. Tails it's me."

They flipped a coin. Ted handed the other stiff his dress coat and suitcase.

"I'll be back in 10 minutes."

They simultaneously activated little buttons on their watches.

241

Ted walked over to the sewer grate, produced a large-model Swiss Army knife, and removed the protective cover. He sniffed the air for a moment, and then disappeared down the newly created opening.

Reagan spoke for another 30 minutes. During that time, the orange cat pranced out of a second sewer grate about 300 feet from the original point of entry.

I never saw Ted above ground again.

Chapter 37
Reagan And The Orange Pussycat

CHAPTER 38

THE DEAD RINGER

Inventions fall into one of three categories: useful, useless, or stupid. The hula-hoop? That's useless, but not very dangerous, so no one actually cares. The little string some guy created to tie around the legs of the barbecued chicken I buy each Saturday? That's stupid: The chicken is dead. It isn't going to run away. (Turkeys - now that's a different matter. Around Thanksgiving, I went to the grocery store. The clerk was the first to give me the bad news: "They all ran out.")

The guy who invented the telephone should be commended. Telephones are useful. The jerk who invented the answering machine? That's a different story. Here's how I'd like him to spend the last 20 seconds of his life.

Ring...Ring

"City Hospital..."

"Cough, cough...thank God. See, I just got bit by a rattlesnake and..."

"All of our operators are busy at the moment but if you'll wait for the next available representative..."

"YOU DON'T UNDERSTAND. THINGS ARE STARTING TO SPIN AND..."

"Your call is important to us, and will be monitored for quality assurance. Here at City Hospital, we strive to offer the best in immediate..."

- - - - - - - - - - - - - - - - - - -

So old. I can remember when people answered their phones at homes and at businesses.

It was 7:30 a.m. Another day at the law office had begun anew. I unlocked the front door, put my briefcase on the desk, and hung up my coat. The phone was already ringing.

"Hello? Law offices."

"Oh! Is this an answering machine?"

"If I say 'yes,' will you believe me?"

"It's 7:30 a.m. in the morning. What are you doing there so early?"

"Answering the phone. By the way, who is this?"

"Julia...Julia Pherdklop...We talked last week about reviewing an apartment lease. Remember?"

"Yes, of course. How can I help you, Mrs. Pherdklop?"

"Well, actually, I just wanted to talk to your answering machine. I wanted to leave a message to have you call me."

"Would you care to talk now?"

"Not really. It's 7:30 in the morning. I've got to get the kids off to school, and it's too early for my mind to function. Could you put me into your voicemail so I can leave you a message?"

The guy who invented *voicemail* ought to be shot, too. I've never found the need to mail my voice anywhere. But I did as Mrs. Pherdklop requested. After all, the customer's always right, and she was as nice a client as any other I never spoke with.

- - - - - - - - - - - - - - - - - - -

Once upon a time, communication wasn't quite so complex. Growing up at my parents' house, we persevered with but one large, heavy, black, party-line rotary phone wired into the living room wall. You could walk three feet in any direction before the black quarter inch cord snapped you back by the neck. What's more, if you needed to crack walnuts, or if a stuck jar lid required loosening, the three pound phone receiver doubled as a hammer.

The good old days are gone forever. Nowadays, if you accidentally drop a cell phone the size of a cigarette lighter on the ground, it self-destructs. But who cares? It's disposable, similar to cameras, voicemail machines, and satellites.

It's the cell phone that has left me in the dust. I don't have one. I pay a receptionist and a secretary to take messages if I'm not around. Or sometimes the message lands in voicemail. But I'll be damned if I'm going to be "on call" 24 hours a day. And to the astonishment of some clients, I do have a private life. I remember one such recent phone conversation.

"O.K., Attorney Fox. Your advice has been helpful. I'll take your cell phone number in case my problems resurface this weekend."

"I don't have a cell phone."

"Yeah, right."

"I don't."

"Why?"

"Because if I did, you might try to call me this weekend."

- - - - - - - - - - - - - - - - - - - -

Some people can no longer function productively unless a cell phone is appended to a portion of their anatomy. Last week I journeyed to the grocery store to buy weekly provisions before the chickens ran out. As I turned to enter the fresh fruit aisle, I spotted the back of a neck belonging to a distinguished bald gentleman who was standing perhaps 100 feet away. He was engaged in an animated conversation with another hairless fellow who was facing him. I put some strawberries in my cart, and moved on.

As I approached, the two fellows came into clearer view. I had been mistaken. There was only one bald man. He was talking to a melon. I inched forward, fearful he might be an escapee from the state hospital. As I passed, I caught sight of the man's cell phone and accompanying earpiece, hidden microphone, and mini-camera.

"But Dear, this one has little brown spots on the top. Can you see them...? That's right, the other melon looks better...Well, Dear, I can't stand here all day. Make up your mind..."

Somewhere out there, about 350 nautical miles above the grocery store, whirled a disposable satellite transmitting all this important data to Mrs. Melonhead back home.

My mother employed a slightly less sophisticated test when purchasing a melon. She knocked on it. If it knocked back, she bought it.

- - - - - - - - - - - - - - - - - - - -

Harvey died - a real gentleman and a good client. Everyone at the law office wanted to attend the funeral, so we put a sign on the door, and walked the three blocks to the service at St. Ursula's Church.

Father Benkowski officiated. The alter was jammed with flowers. The sanctuary was filled to capacity with mourners from all over the Valley. The priest discussed Harvey's many accomplishments during an illustrious lifetime. Despite the multitude of faithful present, every word uttered by the cleric could be heard clearly, for the church possessed acoustics that favored the effortless transmittal of the spoken word to each corner of the massive sanctuary.

"My friends," Father Benkowski entreated, "let us pray."

Everyone silently bowed his or her head.

"We're in the money. We're in the money, da da-da-da-da. We're in the money now!"

Someone three pews in front of me had failed to turn off his cell phone. It must have been important. He took the call. But at least, thank God to whom we were then silently praying, the recipient of the musical message was polite. He whispered into the phone, so the rest of us would not be unduly disturbed. And Harvey probably didn't mind. He was dead.

"What?...I'm in church...Fine...One quart or two?...Skim or whole? O.K., I gotta go..."

There are times when cell phones at funerals actually make sense.

Years ago, at time of interment, the graveside attendants would tie a string to the finger of the decedent reposing in the coffin. When the coffin was lowered into the earth, the string ran above the ground to a small bell hanging at the grave. If the dearly departed was not truly dead and decided to wake up, all he had to do was wiggle his finger, and the dead ringer would be released from his premature tomb. An inexpensive cell phone might be more efficient.

"Hello, Maude."

"Who is this?"

"Calvin...*Your son.*"

"Calvin! Didn't we just bury you on Tuesday?"

"Funniest thing...Apparently, I wasn't dead after all. It was just a nasty cough. Anyway, could you come get me?"

"Calvin! You're fading in and out. Could you roll a little to your left?"

- - - - - - - - - - - - - - - - - - -

Mary Teresa O'Hurley received a new job offer she couldn't refuse. However, it meant moving 1,000 miles away, the loss of her many local friends, and the sale of her beloved house on Chestnut Street. There, she had spent untold hours redesigning the interior of her Tudor home. Only recently had she achieved the decor and ambiance she had for years sought to capture.

She requested that I draft the Agreement of Sale.

"What is the purchase price?" I inquired.

"$340,000," she sighed.

I asked her all the other pertinent questions. Did the dishwasher stay? What about heating fuel left in the basement tank? How many garage door openers were there? I took down all the information.

"Listen, Larry, I'm going on a church retreat next week," she said before leaving. "It's a silent retreat at the nunnery. No one's allowed to talk. But, I gave the realtor your number. If someone puts a bid on the house, she'll contact you while I'm away."

"But what if I need to talk to you directly?"

"That's a tough one. I'll have my cell phone with me to check messages when it vibrates, but I won't be able to speak. I'm sure any interested buyer can wait a week until I get back."

Tuesday morning the phone rang. It was Hilda Flumgartner, famous for carrying her Shih-tzu in her purse. Her dog and flamboyant dress didn't seem to hurt business. She was one of the top-selling realtors in the Valley.

"You just won't believe it," she said, as flustered as usual.

"How are you, Hilda?"

"Listen to this...I got a full-price offer on the O'Hurley Tudor on Chestnut. Mary Teresa told me to call if I had any nibbles."

"That's good news," I agreed. "She'll be back from her retreat next week. Tell the buyer on Monday - "

"No...No...No! You don't understand. The buyers are only here for the next 24 hours. They need to find a place before they fly back to Idaho. It's either this or another Tudor they saw on the west side. Get it?"

She quickly enumerated all the terms and contingencies proposed by the purchasers.

I dialed O'Hurley's cell phone number. Then I engaged in a one-sided conversation.

"Mary, if you are listening, tap once on the mouthpiece of your cell phone."

Tap.

"Good. We need to talk. Please tap once for Yes and twice for No. O.K.?"

Tap.

"The realtor found a buyer at full price. They want to settle in a month. Is that possible?"

Tap.

"Will you be taking the fireplace andirons?"

Tap...Tap...

I asked her several other questions. Never before had I sold a Tudor mansion during a silent retreat, employing a tapping sound by cell phone. The nuns weren't any the wiser, and Mary Teresa didn't break her vow of silence.

Cell phones certainly are a wonderful invention.

Chapter 38
The Dead Ringer

CHAPTER 39

THE INVITATION

Last Thursday, I received an invitation to join AARP. I didn't tell them I had just turned 55. Their spy network registered me without permission. The letter began, "Now that you are decrepit, why not join us? We're gray. We vote, and we're here to stay." I reached for my bifocals. I wanted to land this trash in the basket on the first shot.

I received an invitation to play golf at an upscale course in Coopersburg. My buddies and I figured a new experience would do us good. We even called ahead for a tee-time. As I stood ready to hit my first drive, a young manager came running out of the clubhouse heading my way.

"Hey, Sir?" he said breathlessly.

I stopped mid-swing. "Yes?"

"Are you 55?"

"Yes..." I tentatively volunteered.

The kid was clutching a $1.00 bill in his outstretched hand.

"Then you qualify for our senior citizen discount," he panted. "Here."

It was the first time I had ever benefited as a senior citizen. I had saved one dollar. I was depressed for 18 holes.

Invitations that include the word "cordially" are the most insidious. Some lawyer longs to become a judge, or some politician yearns for more power, and before I know it, I'm *cordially* invited to some $300-a-plate chicken-and-rice dinner at the downtown watering hole. I'd like a new car, but I don't invite strangers to pay for it with an indigestible overpriced meal.

On March 2, 1972, NASA launched the Pioneer 10 spacecraft. Its mission was to pass within 81,000 miles of Jupiter at a speed of 82,000 mph. After this encounter, the

252

vehicle explored the outer regions of our solar system. At 9.5 feet long, the craft carried 11 instruments, including a helium vector magnetometer, plasma analyzer, charger particle detector, cosmic ray telescope, Geiger tube, radiation and meteoroid detector, ultraviolet photometer, imaging photopolarimeter, and infrared radiometer. But these aren't the gadgets that make Pioneer 10 so special. Sooner or later, most Hondas will carry all of it as standard equipment.

No. It's that Pioneer 10 is the first spacecraft to leave our solar system. Soon it will begin to travel unassisted through our galaxy, and in just a few million years, it will leave that realm, and pass into space beyond our Milky Way. It will travel forever past other galaxies, well after our solar system has disappeared and our galaxy has imploded upon itself.

There's something else: Pioneer 10 and her sister ship Pioneer 11 launched on April 5, 1972, both carry invitations, a 6-by-9-inch gold anodized plaque bolted to the main frame of each spacecraft. The invitation looks like this:

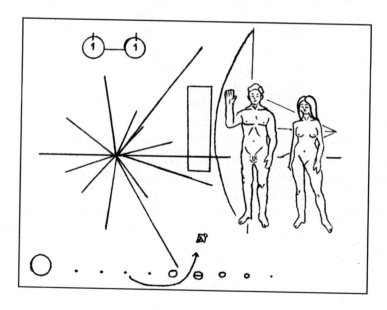

It's designed to induce any quizzical alien who might run across these drifting space vehicles to come visit us. The invitation explains exactly where we live in relation to our sun, and depicts what some of our hair-dos looked like in 1973.

I find it ironic that prior to ever having laid eyes on this NASA-designed diagram, I had a pretty good idea where the earth was located. After all, I was born and raised here. But now that I've studied this intergalactic map, I'm no longer so sure. There are several arrows, but not one of them indicates magnetic north or south. There's a rectangle and an arc next to some bare-ass guy and his extrovertish girlfriend. (By the way, who gave NASA permission to send intergalactic smut? The man and his date are naked. If I sent a postcard like that across town, I'd get busted.) They are both much larger than the earth, which is depicted as one of several various sized circles about as big as a whole wheat cheerio. Nowhere is the New Jersey Turnpike.

I've never met an alien from another galaxy. But if I did, I probably wouldn't like him, her, or it. I'm still not sure the annexation of Alaska and Hawaii was a good idea.

So who the hell told NASA to invite these folks - beings that might have three eyes - in the back of their two heads? Maybe they hate Girl Scouts. The possibilities are endless, and that's how much time they have to get here. It's an open-ended invite. It's just one more thing I have to worry about, and it could have easily been avoided, if the damn plaque, created at taxpayer expense, had remained within the earth's gravitational pull.

All I can hope is that we have something in common with the aliens, and that the recipient of this invitation refuses to let his wife drive. Maybe he'll take a left at Orion instead of a right, and only realize the problem when he hits the Big Dipper.

Chapter 39
The Invitation

CHAPTER 40

LEHIGH VALLEYISMS

I have lived in the Lehigh Valley my entire life, which is no easy feat. From a cartographer's point of view, it doesn't exist. There is a Lehigh Valley Airport that went *international* about the same time the House of Pancakes accepted similar honors. And there is a Lehigh Valley Hospital for the locals who get sick of this place. There's a Lehigh Valley Dairy for cows who graze here, and a Lehigh Valley Chamber of Commerce. But, again, there is no "Lehigh Valley." If it does exist, it's unclear where it is, exactly. Most locals can't seem to agree where it begins and where it ends. Personally, I think it starts about 40 miles north of Philadelphia, and stretches to within 30 miles of the Scranton/Wilkes-Barre metro area, and encompasses all of Allentown, Bethlehem (Bethlum), and Easton. That's important to know, because if you're flying into Lehigh Valley International, your luggage will be ticketed to arrive at "ABE." This is the official airport code depicted on local maps, both aeronautical and geographical. It's my guess that the Lehigh Valley takes in all of Northampton County, Lehigh County, and parts of Berks, Bucks, Monroe, Carbon, and Schuylkill Counties, except where the Delaware Valley exists, but nobody is sure where that place starts and stops, since it isn't depicted on any grid either.

One way to determine if you are in the Lehigh Valley is to listen to the language of its natives. As any outsider knows, there's a definite Lehigh Valley dialect. Unlike any other place in the world, Lehigh Valleyans casually expect foreigners to understand and use this strange form of the English language immediately upon entering the area. Another good reason to learn the Valley's borders.

True Lehigh Valleyans will not find anything from this chapter unusual. In the past, when I have pointed out the use of Lehigh Valleyisms, the locals have looked at me as a

Bendict Arnold. Who dares question the authenticity, the grammatical purity, the historical ethnicity of this spoken word?

I don't mock or ridicule my fellow Lehigh Valley neighbors. Rather, I believe, similar to Margaret Mead, that the traits of unique cultures must be chronicled and memorialized for future generations to study, lest the tribe disappear from the face of the earth, its language, conjugations, and declensions forever lost.

Just as there is no Lehigh Valley, there is no lexicon or dictionary delineating Lehigh Valleyisms. I wish to take the first step in the long journey that rectifies this oversight. By doing so, the foreigner seeking to venture within our borders may consult this reference manual, and prepare ahead of time. It might possibly keep him or her from going *nutzt.*

I have decided, for the moment, not to categorize definitions or phrases in alphabetical order. That will come with the second or third unabridged edition. For now, let's focus on the words, the subtlest nuances, and explain their proper use. Let us begin.

If a Lehigh Valleyan wishes to make an emphatic point reflecting that he is correct and that the person confronted is wrong, this is done by placing hands on hips with vigorous movement of the elbows back and forth, while simultaneously shouting *Lookit.* (For greater emphasis, the word *now* can be inserted first: *Now, lookit!*) Note, however, that the use of the words "now" and "then" has no correlation to the present or the past. Both are, with the above exception, always placed at the end of a sentence. As an example, "now" can be utilized to reach an informal consensus.

Incorrect use: "You remember when that happened?"
Correct use: "You remember when that happened, say now?"

"Then" is utilized primarily by waitresses employed in polished aluminum diners who wish to complete a thought couched in a question.

Incorrect use: "Will that be all?"

Correct use: "Will that be all then?" "You(s) want your checks, then?" (Note that a "check" is not a negotiable instrument tendered by payor to payee. It's the opposite, a bill due and owing.)

Latin plurals are routinely ignored. When in doubt, Lehigh Valleyans just add an "s" to be safe. Common examples include "a plate full of shrimps and spaghettis;" "he shot two deers while missing a flock of sheeps;" "he had his hairs cut." Plurals may be utilized in concert with the second person pronoun, but never in conjunction with the third person.

Incorrect use: "Have you seen those guys?"

Correct use: "Have yous seen them guys?"

Since stores that end in "s" (Sears, Macy's) appear to carry more inventory, most retail names are pluralized to suggest greater selection.

Correct use: "Are you going to the Wal-Marts then, or Kmarts?"

Prepositions are used sparingly. "He shit himself." "I graduated high school." "We shopped Sears." Prepositions that are retained due to the above non-use are usually added to the end of a sentence for no particular reason. "Are you going with?"

When speaking of nourishment, Hebraic phrases may be used both to inquire and respond regarding one's state of hunger:

"Jew eat?

"No. Jew?"

"Not jet."

Generally, dinner is served around suppertime. At such family gatherings, it is acceptable to substitute the letters "dd" for "tt." "May I have a glass of wudder?" "Please pass the budder."

Identification of an individual may be easier when a traumatic event is incorporated within the sentence.

"LeAnn is Donna's husband that died sister."

"That's George whose brother lost his leg's cousin."

The "Rule of 35" applies throughout the Lehigh Valley. If a tributary realizes a flow of less than 35 gallons per minute, it is referred to as a *crick*; 35 gallons or more, it's a *creek*. During a drought, a creek can become a crick. During floods...you get the idea.

If a piece of pottery costs less than $35, it's a *vase*; $35 or more, it becomes a *vaas*. It's a living room *suite* if it costs at least $35, otherwise, it's just a *suit*. Car *radiators* cost less than $35. *Raadiators* cost $35 or more. (A car battery is always pronounced *badtree*. *A carburetor is a carbrater*.)

In the less formal plumbing circles, a spigot is always pronounced "spicket."

Sentences may begin in the past tense, and end in the present. "I was doing that since I am 10."

The word *Philly* can refer to a town, a cigar, a horse, a young woman, or a baseball team. Some natives have been known to use all five connotations in the same paragraph.

Certain words that at first appear to be opposites may nonetheless be used interchangeably.

"That truck was filled with an *inflammable* liquid," or one may shorten things a bit by saying "That truck was filled with a *flammable* liquid." (As a result of the above usage, some gases have been described as *inert*, or if the speaker is out of time, just plain *ert*.)

"She decided to go, *irregardless* of the consequences," may be shortened to *"regardless* of the consequences."

Insects are not always identified by their entomological names, and emphasis may be achieved by adding a syllable. "There were *cockeroaches* all over the house."

Lightning bugs may be pronounced *lightening bugs* or just *fireflies* for short. Centipedes are known as *thousand leggers* even though very few actually have that many feet. Bugs in this location have teeth, since Lehigh Valleyans are always getting *bit*. Luckily, very few inhabitants are ever stung by a dog. Spiderwebs can ultimately become cobwebs, but cobwebs can never be transformed into spiderwebs.

S, T, X, and Z may be interchanged, deleted or added as necessary.

"Once(t) upon a time..."

"He went acrosst the street."

"I smell gaz."

"Can I axt you a question?" (The more acceptable phrase is "May I tap your brain for a minute, if you have one.")

"She was eating xgs for breakfast."

Meteorological descriptions may employ a sense of longing ("They want weather") or use of the vocal cords ("They're calling for rain.") There is some debate as to who "they" actually are.

Phrases dealing with litigation utilize verbs never uttered in a court of law:

"They *inked* the contract."

"The lawsuit was *tossed.*"

"They were able to *squash* the indictment."

There is also the Chinese-soup defense. "Nobody is willfully *wonton* to have an accident."

The difference between "leave, left and let" can be confusing, since the verbs may be utilized interchangeably in both the present and past tense. "Leave me go already;" "Let me go, then;" I *left* out the cat," but "I *let* out the apartment." The use of "get" and "go" can be combined to signify the beginning of a new undertaking. Example: "We worked on that from the getgo." The verb "go" has many connotations:

People don't visit. They *go up to* someone's house.

However, no one ever "goes" to the beach. They're *down the shore.*

Proper utilization of "take" and "give" is even more daunting: "I took a shit," actually refers to the deposit, rather than the removal of matter. "I just don't give a shit," however, does not refer to a state of constipation.

Geese have a special place in Lehigh Valleyisms. Reference is made to them when staring at something, or when feeling cold.

"Well, just take a gander at that!"

"I was so cold I got goosepimples." (Note that goosebumps are, from a dermatological point of view, a larger, longer lasting form of goosepimples. "Goose" is always utilized in its singular non-possessive form, while pimples remains in the plural configuration. As a result, no one ever refers to the condition as "geesepimple" or "goose's pimples").

Sometimes something is missing in its entirety. In such a case, it's not merely "gone" - it's *all* gone.

There are times when it is best to confirm the positive by using the negative.

"Let me see if I can't locate her for you."

"It's so nice to see you again, I don't mind telling ya."

Mutual confirmation of a thought may be memorialized by joining together five words at the end of a sentence.

"It sure is hot, *youknowwhatimean*?

If it's too hot inside, someone will probably *put the air on.*

Things in the Lehigh Valley can, on occasion, be better than exceptional, by inserting the word *mighty*. "That dinner was mighty fine."

Small lineal distances existing between opposite endpoints are described in terms of small animals. Larger distances are described in terms of larger animals:

"The two women sat *kitty* corner from each other."

"The skyscrapers are *catty* corner at the intersection."

Two word phrases may be morphed into one-word abbreviations if no one objects.

Electrical power is often shortened. "Did you get your *electric* hooked up?" *Insurance policies* become one word.

"I just ordered my *insurances*."

Some nouns may also serve as verbs.

"I wouldn't *itch* that scratch if I were you."

If you must leave, sometimes it should be done with emphasis: "Get the *heck* out."

If you have a purpose, dramatic emphasis may be added.

"He was, for all *intensive* purposes, ready to proceed."

A possessive pronoun may be given greater emphasis by merely adding the letter "n" at the end of a sentence.

"This is *yourn*. That's *myan*."

Emphasis may be denoted by use of the phrase *the one*:

"The one day I went for a walk." "Remember the one time you tripped?" "The one lady always does my hair."

The possessive pronoun "my" should, whenever possible, be utilized in place of the article "the":

"The cleaning lady always scrubs my sink." "He does all my shopping for me."

Assaults never take place in a downward motion. Correct confession: "I hit him upside the head." Hearing the spoken word takes the same direction. "Now listen up, youse guys."

Lehigh Valleyans never *vacuum*. "I swept the house."

Distance is always converted into time. Question: "How far is it to Bethlum?" Answer: "20 minutes."

- - - - - - - - - - - - - - - - - - -

If you have utilized any of the following phrases in conversation, you are probably a Lehigh Valley native:

"The roof is O.K., but the *chimbley* is cracked."

"We worked overtime at the *Bethlum* Steel for extra *insentative* pay."

"I can remember just about anything, 'cause I got a *photogenic* memory."

"Grandma is *icening* the birthday cake."

"They were playing a game of *badmitton*."

"It was valuable, so I put it in the safety-posit box."

"Do you have any mail going to the mailbox?"

"That'll learn ya."

"She was suffering from a detached rectum." (Either way, it's got to hurt.)

"I got to go."

I've found that analyzing Lehigh Valleyisms is a lot like buying a can claiming to contain evaporated milk. Sometimes it's best to simply accept what's said on faith without too much introspection.

Chapter 40
Lehigh Valleyisms